BUMMER & LAZARUS

San Francisco's Famous Dogs

Contemporary illustrations by
Edward Jump

Compiled and with a new introduction by
Malcolm E. Barker

LONDONBORN PUBLICATIONS SAN FRANCISCO 2001

First printed December, 2000
10 9 8 7 6 5 4 3 2 1

Londonborn Publications
P.O. Box 77246, San Francisco, CA
94107-0246
www.sanfranciscomemoirs.com

Library of Congress Cataloging-in-Publication Data
Bummer & Lazarus: San Francisco's famous dogs : revised
with new stories, new photographs, and new introduction /
contemporary illustrations by Edward Jump ; compiled and
introduced by Malcolm E. Barker.
    p. cm.
Includes bibliographical references (p.).
ISBN 0-930235-07-X (alk. Paper)
    1. Bummer (Dog) 2. Lazarus (Dog) 3. Dogs—Califor-
nia—San Francisco—Biography. 4. San Francisco (Calif.)
—History—19th century. I. Jump, Edward. II. Barker,
Malcolm E., 1933-

SF426.2.B85 2000

636.7'009794'61—dc21   00-048384

Separating myth from reality

Now out of print, the first edition of this little book has been hailed as a minor classic, and its heroes have been further memorialized with a large brass plaque at the base of one of San Francisco's most famous landmarks. Meanwhile, I confess to a researcher's obsession with uncovering the whole story: This new volume not only recounts the engaging history of Bummer and Lazarus but solves the mystery of what ultimately became of the two canine companions. Along the way it also introduces several other dogs well-known to nineteenth century San Franciscans but since forgotten.

It is 140 years since Bummer and Lazarus roamed the streets of San Francisco, yet their names are still recalled with affection by local citizens. They have become legends. As with many legends, their story is now a blend of truths, half-truths, and far-fetched fabrications. Conflicting accounts litter dozens of books and hundreds of articles published worldwide. Some of these are now circulating on the Internet.

The original story is simple enough. Bummer and Lazarus were strays and acknowledged no master. They lived in the early 1860s and gained the respect and attention of the people because of their expertise at killing rats and their unique bond of friendship. Newspapers constantly reported their escapades, whether it was stealing a bone from another dog or stopping a runaway horse. City supervisors exempted them from a strict ordinance that banned dogs downtown unless they had a leash and/or muzzle. When Lazarus died, one newspaper ran a lengthy obituary entitled "Lament for Lazarus." While Bummer lay dying, the local papers vied with each other in updating the news, and Mark Twain added his characteristically caustic commentary.

From these facts a number of myths have evolved. The most persistent is that the dogs belonged to Joshua Abraham Norton, a local character who, from 1859 through January, 1880, roamed the city claiming to be Emperor Norton I of the United States and Protector of Mexico. Yet of all the contemporary newspaper accounts of Bummer and Lazarus, not one mentioned Norton. Similarly, in twenty years of newspaper stories about Norton, not one mentioned the dogs. The earliest account of such a liaison that I have found was published in Germany in 1886—21 years after Bummer died. The author, Theodor Kirchhoff, did not arrive in San Francisco until four years after Bummer's death.

The most likely explanation is that people who arrived in the city after the dogs died saw a series of cartoons depicting them with the emperor and assumed that these represented the truth. Since then, generations of storytellers and writers have repeated these assumptions. In reality, these cartoons, drawn by Edward Jump, were intended as satirical commentaries about famous personalities of the day. One personality who was not amused was Norton. He became so incensed when he saw in a store window an illustration of himself eating with Bummer and Lazarus that he struck the window with his cane, and broke the cane. *The indignity of it—he, an emperor, eating with stray dogs...!* This incident, combined with any lack of substantiation in contemporary accounts, would surely seem to negate any possibility of kinship.

Another myth that has been perpetuated since the late 1800s is that three seats were reserved on opening nights of new shows—one each for Emperor Norton, Bummer, and Lazarus. The idea of reserving theater seats for dogs is far-fetched even by the standards of 1860s San Francisco. Nevertheless, I searched reviews and countless books about the city's early theaters in the fruitless hope of learning how the story originated.

My time was not wasted. In the announcement for an 1862 musical farce I found Bummer and Lazarus listed in the cast. There was no indication that they showed up for their performance. (See page 30.)

One of Jump's most famous cartoons depicts a procession of identifiable politicians, businessmen and others attending the funeral of Lazarus. Norton gives the blessing, a small drummer boy swings a rat as if it were incense, and Bummer looks on, mournfully. (See page 32.) To the artist, this was merely another satire on the times. To future observers, however, it represented more than a figment of Jump's creative imagination. Stories began circulating that Lazarus had been buried, and that hundreds of local dignitaries had attended the funeral.

In his 1886 account, Kirchhoff elaborated by saying that the funeral was arranged by the dog's "imperial master" (implying

Norton), and that it had "a following of many people on foot and in carriages." Furthermore, he mistakenly identified the event as Bummer's funeral instead of Lazarus'.

The story was given credibility by an entry in the venerable *Guinness Book of World Records* that proclaimed an estimated 10,000 people attended the greatest dog funeral on record.

The truth is that Bummer and Lazarus were not buried. When they died their skins were stuffed by a taxidermist and displayed in the two saloons they frequented while alive. I pointed this out to Norris D. McWhirter, the *Guinness* editor in London. In his reply, he wrote:

> Alas, [fiction] has no place between our covers and therefore we will have to regretfully excise it from the next printings and face the wroth of those who will inevitably write to us asking why we have moved one

of their favourite entries.

In an effort to keep Bummer and Lazarus in *Guinness*, I submitted an 1863 account in which they are reported to have killed "over 400 rats" when the gallery of a local fruit market was cleared. (See page 35.) I suggested this would make them the greatest ratters on record. But the names Bummer and Lazarus were expunged from the book, apparently not to be seen there again.

For me, the most intriguing mystery was the fate of the stuffed skins. I had heard that they were displayed at the Golden Gate Park museum and then destroyed by the 1906 earthquake and fire. Attempting to verify this, I searched all entries prior to December, 1904, in the museum's massive, hand-written inventory books, but found no reference to Bummer and Lazarus.

Shortly after the first edition of this book was published in 1984, however, reader

Michael Rosen sent me a clipping from the *Daily Morning Call* for February 2, 1906, with the headline "Bummer and Lazarus in the Park Museum." The account read:

> Wednesday D.B. White, 425 Sansome street, gave "Bummer" and "Lazarus" to the Golden Gate Park Museum. Commissioner Reuben H. Lloyd, who knew the dogs in the "sixties," accepted the donation on behalf of the commission, and Professor Gruber at once installed the new exhibit.

Armed with this, I returned to the museum and checked the inventory book for 1906. Sure enough, the skins were received in February. They were transferred to the Department of Natural History. A further notation adds that they were in the janitor's loft. A single word was scribbled in the margin: "Destroyed." There is no mention about Professor Gruber installing the new exhibit.

I looked at the clipping, then at the inventory item, and back again at the clipping. Only then did I realize their full significance. The address of the donor—425 Sansome Street—was the same as that of the saloon Pless & Martin. An earlier newspaper account had confirmed that in 1892 the skin of Lazarus was still at 425 Sansome, and that the skin of Bummer was at the former location of Martin & Horton's saloon, at the corner of Montgomery and Clay.

For me, this seemed to be the end of the story. But I was wrong! The skins languished, unseen, at the museum another four years. In April, 1910, the *San Francisco Chronicle* reported that "while rummaging in the storeroom" the curator "came across the stuffed bodies of Bummer and Lazarus, two Fire Department dogs of this city in the early sixties." The report added that the curator was "restuffing" and preparing them for exhibition in the natural history department.

I first became fascinated with Bummer and Lazarus in 1966, five years after I immigrated to San Francisco from England. My fascination has not dimmed in the intervening 35 years. If anything, it has intensified. Since 1984 I have been campaigning to grant these two dogs their own chapter in the city's colorful history, separate from that of Emperor Norton. (It has been suggested that having a name like Barker may account for this obsession!)

The newspaper accounts you will find in this book were written by journalists who knew Bummer and Lazarus. The charming story they tell deserves to stand alone, without the grossly exaggerated elements that have been added since.

I do realize that a story's appearance in a newspaper does not mean without a doubt that it is true. Also, I am aware that the style in which some of these accounts were written indicates that the writers were unashamedly stretching the truth to add color to an otherwise insignificant event. To me, these embellishments are more acceptable than those that were added later because they belong to the period; they provide us with a glimpse into mid-nineteenth century humor and tolerance. They become facets in the kaleidoscope that was San Francisco in the mid-1860s.

Bummer and Lazarus were not the only dogs whose antics were reported in the newspapers, but they certainly had more coverage than others. Before December, 1866, fires in San Francisco were fought by volunteer firemen attached to a number of individual companies. Many of these companies had dogs that were written about in the local press. The following appeared in the *Alta* on February 13, 1865, under the headline "Death of a Notable Animal."

"Jack," the famous half-mastif, half-bull-dog who has long "ran with the machine" and lodged in the house of California Engine Co., No. 4, for twelve years, died on Friday night, and his skin is now in the hands of the taxidermist, who will prepare it for occupying a place in the company meeting room for the future. "Jack" was a character and almost as well known in his particular line as old "Bummer" himself.

He never paid the slightest attention to street rows or the ringing of bells for anything but a fire, but the first tap of the alarm bell or the rolling of an engine through the streets set him off half crazy with excitement, and he would, if outside, run at once to the house of No. 4 and commence springing against the door to attract the attention of those within.

He had a habit of dashing into a burning building and seizing whatever came in his way, with a view to rescuing it from destruction, and to that habit fell a victim at last, dying from injuries inflicted by some stranger at the Market street fire some two months since. He was deservedly a favorite with No. 4 and one of the pets of the Department.

Question: Did this 1865 account of Jack's death become confused with accounts of Bummer's death a few months later and, subsequently, inspire the following account that appeared in *The Argonaut* in 1882? Furthermore, did either one (or both) of these inspire the story that Bummer was a firefighters' pet and was killed at a fire—a story that today circulates on the Internet?

Bummer grew very stout, and one night, being seized with a fit of curiosity on the subject of fires, he accompanied the engines to South Park, where a conflagration was going on. There were a number of buildings burned; the excitement was great; in an evil moment Bummer, who had so far forgotten himself as to become excited too, got in the way of the hose, and was thrown over, trampled on, and killed, being no longer quick or agile enough in his movements to get out of the way in time to save himself. . . . For some days, if not weeks, the unhappy [Lazarus] did not appear in public; he must have remained in seclusion during the day, and issued forth at night into streets as dreary and deserted as his own altered life.

Meantime, the fire company, . . . recognizing in him a public hero, had his skin stuffed and mounted in their engine room in such an extremely natural manner as to elicit much admiration. On the occasion of a civic display very soon afterward, this company "turned out," and, mounted on a stand, poor Bummer's vivid effigy accompanied them in parade.

The day chosen chanced to be one on which poor Lazarus had ventured forth, a wretched ghost of his former self. On reaching Montgomery Street he met the pageant, and, raising his sad eyes, beheld his former patron's figure carried aloft before the engine. The howl he uttered is said by those who heard it to have been blood-curdling. It was the last sound he was ever known to make, for, raising his head higher than he had ever held it before, he seemed mutely to appeal to heaven against such mummery, and then started homeward, never more to appear in the theatre of San Francisco affairs. When, on the removal of some rubbish on the corner of Leidesdorff Street, his remains were discovered, no one was by to suggest a taxidermist; but that may not have been from lack of good feeling as much as from the necessity for chloride of lime.

Thus are myths generated!

Napoleon, and
Chuffy the Chain Gang Dog

Most of the dogs that appeared in the press during this period rated only one account, usually a glowing obituary. Some of these tell of funerals, while others state bluntly that the bodies had been handed over to the taxidermist—not an uncommon practice with favored pets in those days.

A rare eyewitness account of a dog's funeral in the mid-1860s appeared in the *Bulletin* in January, 1914. James H. Wilkins recalled the funeral of Napoleon, a performing dog that belonged to circus owner John Wilson. Napoleon was already old when he and his master retired from show business and settled in San Francisco during the 1860s. Wilkins wrote:

> Though he never enjoyed the notoriety of Bummer and Lazarus, Napoleon nevertheless was a favorite with great numbers of pioneers, and a well-known figure on Montgomery Street. . . . The funeral of "Lazarus," as I have heard it described, was something of a burlesque. The funeral of Napoleon was the real thing. I know, because I attended it in person and never have witnessed a ceremony more marked and impressive in solemn, sympathetic setting.

Wilkins went on to say that the funeral was attended by more than a hundred sincere sympathizers including bankers, lawyers, stockbrokers and "perhaps a clergyman or so, together with a miscellaneous assortment of sorrow-laden sports." The funeral address was given by John W. Dwinelle, the lawyer after whom Dwinelle Hall on the University of California's Berkeley campus was named. The grave site was "a lonely spot on Russian Hill."

Chuffy the Chain Gang Dog was another

contemporary of Bummer and Lazarus. He earned this title by his close association with convicted chicken thief Francisco Fuentes. According to the Christmas Day, 1859, *Daily Alta California*, this "poor little nondescript animal" was a familiar sight as his master and other manacled prisoners labored in Washington Square.

> Ups and downs he certainly has had, as instanced in the halting gait of the poor quadruped, produced by an accident which unfortunately cut off one of his feet. This gives him a sort of "step-and-fetch-it" gait, which, together with his "sad-dog" look, makes him wear a most lackadaisical appearance. . . . Chuffy has been the innocent but devoted attendant of Francisco in all his midnight forays, and we presume keeps watch for his master while the latter is engaged in his unlawful calling. As fast as the Sonorian is detected, and sentenced to the public works, Chuffy seems to understand the matter, and considers himself as likewise in durance vile, regularly accompanying his unworthy proprietor to his daily labor, sitting about in convenient places during working hours and contentedly following the old sinner and his ball-and-chain companions back again to the Station House at evening.
>
> In the prison the dog is a recognized character. He is always promptly on hand at feeding time, and quietly picks the bones thrown to him. Being of diminutive dimensions, he has easy ingress and egress under the Station House door, but never gets far enough away to miss accompanying the procession, wending its way toward Washington Square for the daily routine of labor.
>
> Chuffy has few canine acquaintances. Either in his simple innocence he imagines the chain gang to be some intensely exclusive and aristocratic institution—a privileged class with whom the common people

about the streets are not worthy to associate—and thus his connection with them places him a peg above other dogs; or the rest of the Trays, Blanches and Sweethearts scent the real plebian and eschew his company. Certain it is, Chuffy enjoys a monopoly of the chain gang favors, and not another cur presumes to court a quarrel with him. He has sagacity worthy a better master; but, poor brute, he is quite satisfied with his lot.

Two Cribs, a Jack, and "Jenny Lind"

The police department also had pet dogs. In December, 1866, the *Alta* led its City Items column with this:

> For the past 15 years a crop-eared yellow dog known as "Crib" (short for "Cribbage"), has been the pet of the police and one of the most heavy taxes on the proprietors of the lunch tables around the City Hall. "Crib's" origin is involved in doubt and obscured by the mists of time, but there is a dim tradition that he was born in the City Prison and of disreputable parentage; but, however that may be, he was among the characters of San Francisco and, next to "Bummer" and "Lazarus," the greatest of our canine specialties.
>
> Affectionate to a degree when hungry, he would fawn upon and dance about anybody who seemed disposed to give him a dinner, and when full fed would not hesitate to bite the hand of his benefactor, or any other man who came near him and attempted to caress him. Whether this peculiarity was native to him, or the result of vile associations, it is impossible to say, but public opinion inclines strongly towards the latter theory. As "Crib" grew old, a tendency to scorbutic and cutaneous disease was developed in him, and for some years his back had presented the appearance of having been burned over by a prairie fire and badly harrowed down and seeded over again.

On the first day of December, 1866, in the gray dawn of the morning, a policeman found "Crib" in the agonies of death, and half an hour later he was subject for the Coroner. Whether he died from grief at the wholesale slaughter of his offspring which was about to be perpetuated by order of the Police Commissioners, committed suicide by taking an overdose of Kenney's hard boiled corned beef rather than be shot at by the policemen who so distinguished themselves at the last target excursion of the National Guard at the Encinal de Alameda, or was basely murdered through the medium of a ready made sausage by somebody who wished to get even on the police in advance for the butchery of their pets, is as yet unknown: but certain it is, he sleeps the sleep of the just, and has gone to his reward, whatever and wherever that may be.

His funeral will take place in a day or two, under the joint auspices of the Reporters for the Press, the members of the Police Court bar, and the proprietors of 210 saloons within half a block of the City Hall.

Apparently Crib and Jack were not uncommon names for dogs in those days. In April, 1863, the firefighters of Manhattan Fire Engine Company lowered their flag to half staff in remembrance of their Crib, who died of lung congestion the morning after attending a fire on Powell Street.

Earlier, firefighters of Manhattan No. 2 Company mourned the death by poisoning of their 2½-year-old Scottish terrier, Jack. "The taxidermist has received orders to stuff his skin, and Jack, albeit with a pair of glass eyes, will continue to watch over the interests of his good friends and true," said the *Bulletin*.

"Jenny Lind," described by the *Alta* as "the celebrated black and tan terrier slut," was considered "an old pioneer" when she died in March, 1864. She was a dog of the world, having crossed the Atlantic three times. Named in honor of a popular singer of the day, she arrived in the city with her master Ebenezer Niles during the Gold Rush. When Niles died, "Jenny Lind" declined numerous offers of a comfortable home and, instead, chose to live at the Blue Wing Saloon. She died there at the age of 15. The *Alta* assured its readers she had not been poisoned, but had died "at peace with all the world from sheer old age."

San Rafael, California   M.E.B.
October, 2000

In October, 1985, Bruce L. Johnson, Library Director of the California Historical Society, found a photograph of the stuffed skins of Bummer and Lazarus in an old scrapbook. He wrote and asked whether I would be interested in seeing it. The stuffed Lazarus did not surprise me. He was almost exactly as described in the *Daily Evening Bulletin* in 1863—"bright and erect" with a "vigilant expression in his eye, as though he smelt a rat." However, Bummer was a pathetic sight, a far cry from Jump's charming drawings. On reflection, that also should not have surprised me, because, whereas Lazarus was poisoned in the prime of life, Bummer died a slow, painful death. According to the newspapers, Bummer never recovered from the loss of his companion and moped along Montgomery Street, staying close to the spot where Lazarus had died. Consequently, by the time Bummer was taken to the taxidermist, he had lost the air of arrogance he had effected while the two friends were the pets of San Francisco.

Courtesy: The California Historical Society

Today, the 853-foot Transamerica Pyramid rises in the neighborhood where, 140 years ago, Bummer and Lazarus were wont to roam. At its base is a tiny park shaded by redwood trees—a popular site where local business folk spend their lunchtimes strolling, reading, or simply basking in the serenity. The park is also where Bummer and Lazarus are best remembered. On March 28, 1992, a 30" x 20" brass plaque recalling their adventures and misadventures was installed at the base of the skyscraper by E Clampus Vitus, a fraternal group dedicated to preserving oftentimes neglected Western history. Richard Avanzino, then president of the San Francisco Society for the Prevention of Cruelty to Animals, introduced two dogs who were seeking homes and had been christened Bummer the 4,732nd and Lazarus the 3,815th.

FAMOUS DOGS HAVE THEIR DAY

EXAMINER/KURT ROGERS

San Francisco's *famed 19th century canine charac-*
ters, Bummer and Lazarus, renowned for stopping
carriages and begging freebies at local saloons, were
honored with a plaque Saturday at the Transamerica
Pyramid. Joining the celebration, sponsored by the
fraternal group E Clampus Vitus, were Bummer the
4,732nd and Lazarus the 3,815th, currently up for
adoption at the Society for the Prevention of Cruelty
for Animals. That's SPCA President Richard Avan-
zino at the other end of the leashes.

Acknowledgements

I am grateful to the following for help in revising this book: Jackie Pels, Hardscratch Press, for editing the new material; David R. Johnson, Hardscratch Press, for creating the cover and title page; Peter Browning, Great West Books, for invaluable help during the final stages of production; Claudine Chalmers for providing information about Edward Jump; and to Susan Moore, Werner Pels, Kevin Mullen, and Gary Sterling. In addition, I thank Tanya Hollis at the California Historical Society, Patricia Keats at the Society of California Pioneers, the library staff at the San Francisco History Center at the San Francisco Public Library, and the staff at the San Francisco Public Library's newspaper room.

Bibliography

The following sources apply to the new material. The principal bibliography begins on page 79.

Brooks, Fred Emerson. "Bummer and Lazarus," *Overland*, volume 58, July- December 1911.

Chalmers, Claudine. *Splendide Californie! Impressions of the Golden State by French Artists 1786-1900*. The Book Club of California, San Francisco. 2000.

Kirchhoff, Theodor. "Californische Kulturbilder" (1886), translated by Rudolph Jordan, Jr., in *Quarterly of The Society of California Pioneers*, volume V, number 4, San Francisco. December 1928.

Parker, Joan. "Two Dogs Who Ruled A City," *California Monthly*, December 1968.

Guinness Book of World Records, The. London. 1983 and 1985.

Argonaut, volume X, number 4. San Francisco. January 28, 1882.

Daily Alta California. San Francisco. 12-25-1859; 4-4-1863; 3-4-1864; 2-13-1865; 12-2-1866.

Daily Evening Bulletin. San Francisco. 3-14-1860; 10-26-1863; 11-25-1893; 1-3-1914.

Daily Morning Call. San Francisco. 7-3-1892; 2-2-1906.

San Francisco Chronicle. 4-11-1910.

"There wasn't a soul on the Coast,
　　From the hoodlum 'way up to the Mayor,
Who did not claim friendship, and boast
　　He had petted and been the purveyor
To Bummer and Lazarus."

Fred Emerson Brooks, 1911

BUMMER & LAZARUS

SAN FRANCISCO'S FAMOUS DOGS

Acknowledgments

Thank you for making available the resource material—

Gladys Hansen, City Archivist, San Francisco Public Library; Grace E. Baker, Librarian, The Society of California Pioneers; Virginia Mann, Senior Registrar, the M.H. de Young Memorial Museum; Janet Ing, Librarian, Albert M. Bender Collection, Mills College, Oakland; Grace A. Evans, Wells Fargo Bank History Department; Irene M. Moran and Lawrence Dinnean at The Bancroft Library, University of California, Berkeley; Beverly Denenberg, Curator, and Bruce Johnson, Library Director, at the California Historical Society. Also, the anonymous but helpful staff members at The Bancroft Library, The General Library at the University of California, Berkeley, The San Francisco Public Library, and the California Historical Society.

Thank you for guidance, assistance and support in the actual production of this book—

Don Greame Kelley and Susan Acker (Feathered Serpent Press, San Rafael), Pat Young (Hillside Setting, Novato), Dick and Jane Murdock (Marin Self-Publishers Association), Dino Bevilaqua (senior photo technician, U.C. Berkeley), Ronald Surtz, Carlo G. Carlucci, James B. Tyler, Judi Larkin, Bill Larkin, John De Bonis, Edward L. Crossley, and Herbert Vanek.

I also want to record my indebtedness to Samuel Clemens and the many anonymous reporters who knew Bummer and Lazarus, and who wrote about them in their newspapers. Without these reports I could not have compiled this book!

M.E.B.

"... two dogs with but a single bark,
two tails that wagged as one ..."

Daily Evening Bulletin, *October 26, 1863*

About This Book

The story of Bummer and Lazarus appears twice in this book.

First it is written as a narrative recalling the highlights of their lives and adventures.

Then the story unfolds as it did for San Franciscans reading their newspapers between 1861 and 1865. Setting this scene is a contemporary account of Montgomery Street, where most of the events occurred.

The illustrations were drawn by Edward Jump and "S.Nooks, Jr." to be sold either as individual lithographs or as letter sheets— writing paper bearing scenes of current events.

A glossary explains certain words, phrases and events which may not be too familiar to readers today. A bibliography lists sources of all references.

Contents

Illustrations

*The name ''S.Nooks, Jr.'' on this is probably a pseudonym. The lithograph was issued by George Holbrook Baker, a popular artist of that period.

All others are by Edward Jump.

Courtesy: The Bancroft Library, University of California

Introduction

Several years ago I became intrigued with the story of Emperor Norton I of the United States, Protector of Mexico, who "reigned" for twenty-one years (1859-1880) in San Francisco. I spent months in the public library reading the local newspapers of the period, following the movements of Joshua Abraham Norton, who had lost his senses after a series of business ventures failed. Like those early San Franciscans, I read how he went about town issuing proclamations, taxing businesses, eating free in restaurants, and traveling to and from the capital at Sacramento, where he attended meetings of the State Legislature.

In those same newspapers I read about two dogs that roamed the streets of the city between 1861 and 1865. They were strays, and ugly, and obeyed nobody. Yet stories about them kept appearing in the papers—even though at the same time thousands of other strays were being thrown into the pound and killed.

Emperor Norton was in the public eye for twenty-one years; Bummer and Lazarus for only five. Whereas today's newspapers often retell Norton's story in detail, they usually dismiss the dogs in a few words, often linking them with Norton. Nowhere do I find any contemporary account making such a connection. I believe they had no more royal affiliation than did the dozen or so other characters who were tolerated by their fellow San Franciscans in those days: people like The Guttersnipe, George Washington II, The Money King, The Great Unknown, Oofty Goofty, and The Fat Boy.

Undoubtedly what has caused the confusion are the numerous lithographs drawn by Edward Jump, a young French-born caricaturist who was living in California at the time. Although Jump also drew many of the other notabilities, he invariably gave prominence to the Emperor and the two dogs. His most famous drawing depicts Norton eating at the free lunch counter of one of the local saloons, while Bummer and Lazarus stand nearby, obviously hoping to share the feast. The Emperor was not amused when he saw it displayed in the window of a stationery store for, according to a report in the *Daily Alta California* on February 14, 1863,

he let fly his walking stick at the window pane and smashed—his stick. The window glass being the stronger, did not break, and the owner of the store coming to the door to quell the disturbance, His Imperial Majesty stalked off with his usual dignity—in his hand holding the balance of power in the shape of a broken cane.

The dogs' regular beat was the area bordered by Washington, Sansome, Sacramento and Kearny streets which, in those days, was the heart of the city. The City Hall was on Kearny, facing Portsmouth Square, in a building that had once housed the Jenny Lind Theater. The major shops and theaters were there, as were several newspaper offices and a number of popular saloons.

Although nobody claimed ownership there are clues suggesting that their principal protector was Mr. Frederick Martin, of Pless & Martin, a saloon located at 425 Sansome Street. This saloon was popular with artists and newspaper men, and an ideal milieu in which to observe and discuss the antics of Bummer and Lazarus.

It is eighteen years since I first read those old newspapers at the San Francisco Public Library, yet the dogs still haunt me. Recently I returned to the archives, this time widening my search to include—among other sources—The Bancroft Library at the University of California, Berkeley, The Society of California Pioneers, the M.H. de Young Memorial Museum, and the California Historical Society. I am even more convinced the story deserves telling on its own without any help from the Emperor.

My dilemma has been in how to present it. To me, the charm is not only in what the dogs did, but also in how the journalists of the day responded. Obviously they enjoyed these assignments, and gave rein to their imagination while keeping their tongues firmly in their cheeks. As a writer, I delight in the way they often played with words—especially when they would tweak Latin or French words and phrases to suit their needs. In this respect I am particularly indebted to Carlo G. Carlucci, author of *A Field Guild to Greek Metre,* (Atypical Press, 1978) for translating the Latin passages and thus uncovering several amusing puns which add another dimension to the contemporary newspaper accounts. The translations are listed by page number in the glossary, beginning on page 75.

To lump the individual reports together without a thread would be confusing since many of the incidents were not reported until the obituaries. Any attempt to retell the story with modern embellishments and pseudo-psychology would rob a lot of the charm. My decision has been to present two versions in the hope the reader will gain the gist of the story through the straightforward narrative in the first part of this book, and then read the actual accounts in the order they appeared in the newspapers more than one hundred years ago. To maintain the flavor of the period I have chosen not to adapt the idiosyncratic mode of nineteenth century spelling to our twentieth century standard, nor to tamper with the inconsistencies to be found within some of these reports.

However, I have restricted the selection to only reports that appeared during the dogs' lifetimes and a few years beyond, and use as my criterion the axiom I learned as a cub reporter in England: "If in doubt, leave out." For readers and researchers interested in studying later reports—some of which conflict blatantly with certain easily verifiable details—I list in the bibliography all resources known to me at this time.

Mill Valley, California
April, 1984   M.E.B.

4

THE STORY. . .

In January, 1861, there was a vicious street fight in San Francisco between two unevenly matched dogs. While people stood by watching, the larger animal bit the smaller one's leg, almost severing it. Nearby was another dog—Bummer, who was already famous in the neighborhood as a champion rat-catcher. When he heard the snarling and the barking he came to investigate, and promptly dashed into the fray to rescue the injured creature. The bully ran off, yelping. Bummer escorted the poor animal to a safe doorway where the two of them slept every night until the injured leg was fully recovered.

From this incident evolved a friendship which was to last as long as the two dogs lived: a friendship which has since become a part of San Francisco's history.

For several days Bummer wandered in and out of the saloons along Montgomery and Clay streets gathering food from the numerous people he had befriended. The only difference from his normal routine was that, instead of eating it there, he carried the food to where his friend lay, to share with him. Eventually the other dog—now named Lazarus—regained his strength and was able to accompany Bummer on his rounds. The two became inseparable, and whenever a nest of rats was uncovered both would be there to fight side by side.

The city was infested with rats. But it was also infested with dogs: "skinny, mangy curs, often times imported from China—creatures without hair and with skeleton tails—living anatomies, their polished scaly sides glistening in the sun, like those of lizards," according to one contemporary report. Only a few years earlier the citizens of this Gold Rush town had taken the law into their own hands by forming vigilance groups to judge and execute criminals. In a similar manner the people now began leaving poisoned food in the streets in an effort to get rid of the dogs.

In spite of this the newspapers continued to relate how San Franciscans took two of these strays—Bummer and Lazarus—to their hearts. Nowhere do we read that either one was attractive to look at. In fact, the papers seem to have delighted in saying how ugly they were. On reflection, it appears they had only two redeeming qualities: their expertise in killing rats and their fascinating bond of friendship.

Stories of their origins are vague and conflicting. One report said Bummer was born on the Western prairies, and that he fought Indians on his way to California; that he lost his master, became demoralized, and spent a short while in Sac-ramento before making his way to San Francisco. A report in the *Daily Morning Call,* July 3, 1892, said that he was brought to the city by an *Alta* reporter, Edward C. Knight, who found him in Petaluma, but that he later wandered off on his own. He was described as Newfoundland, with protruding teeth, a permanent grin, and a clumsy walk.

Even less is known of Lazarus' background, other than the fact he was probably one of the oldest dogs in town, and that he was of a yellowish-black color. We get a better idea of what they looked like by studying a number of lithographs drawn by a famous caricature artist of the day, Edward Jump. These were sold either as individual lithographs or as letter sheets—a nineteenth century variation of the post card.

Bummer was a loner, relishing the status

he had earned for himself, and, until he met up with Lazarus, quite content to make casual acquaintances with people rather than with other dogs. Then he changed his habits dramatically, treating very seriously his newly acquired responsibility as protector and provider. Lazarus, however, was not always as loyal. He was said to be sly, and not adverse to eating a good portion from a bone before taking it to Bummer to share. And the newspapers were quick to report that, when someone shot Bummer in the leg, causing him to mope about in corners, Lazarus coolly deserted him and went off to find another benefactor, not returning until Bummer was well enough to take him around the saloons again. Yet Bummer, being Bummer, showed no signs of recrimination, and was happy to be reunited with his friend. It was the only time they parted company voluntarily, although fate and circumstances were to separate them on a number of occasions.

Meanwhile the problem of strays was becoming more intolerable, and the city Supervisors were compelled to pass (in April, 1862) a strict ordinance prohibiting dogs without a muzzle or leash on any street north of Ninth and east of Larkin. The Poundkeeper was ordered to round them up and take them to the pound where, if they were not redeemed for $5, they were to be executed. The police were authorized to shoot them on sight. Fifty cents would be paid for any dog taken to the pound by the public—a reward that encouraged small boys to take dogs out of the safety of gardens and carry them to the pound. Each week after that the newspapers gave the figures from the Poundmaster's report: 50 impounded and 5 redeemed the first week; 94 impounded and 7 redeemed the second week; and so on. On June 3, the *Alta* gave the total for the first month: 255 impounded and 20 redeemed.

Even while the new ordinance was being drafted, several people became concerned about Bummer and Lazarus. Since they did not have a master, who would provide muzzles and who would remove them at meal times? For a while it certainly seemed they were immune. Furthermore, Bummer's name was applied to a poem published in the *Daily Evening Bulletin,* pleading for leniency for other less fortunate dogs. The poem was entitled "Cur Non?"

However, it was not long before the unthinkable happened: an over-zealous Poundkeeper picked up Lazarus and took him off to the pound along with numerous other strays. Someone paid the $5 for his release, and within a few days hundreds of signatures were attached to a petition calling upon the Board of Supervisors to exempt Bummer and Lazarus specifically from the ordinance. The petition spoke in glowing terms of the service they did for the city as rat-catchers, and added:

> But your petitioners rely especially upon the general affection felt for these two animals, on account of the lessons of protection and faithful association their union has presented for two years past—and in all earnestness pray the consecration of these two dogs as city property, to wander unmolested in pursuit of their daily food.

When the city fathers met on the evening of June 17, 1862, Bummer and Lazarus were seen crouched together outside the chamber, causing another reporter to end his report with this comment:

> If any man carried them there, it was a cute dodge to get favorable action on their petition; if they went there voluntarily, they ought to have free run of the town during the rest of their lives.

The next day there was a great parade and celebration in San Francisco marking the 87th anniversary of the Bunker Hill Battle. There was also a general feeling that the Civil War was almost over, and the people made of this a very patriotic, pro-Union demonstration. For the two dogs, who had recently acquired the nicknames Damon and Pythias (the names of two Pythagorean philosophers of the fourth century B.C. whose steadfast friendship for each other had become proverbial), the general excitement could have been in their honor.

The following week they showed their appreciation by chasing and stopping a runaway horse and cart on Clay Street. At first Bummer ran along one side of the street while Lazarus ran along the other. At Kearny Bummer ran in front of the horse and slowed it down until a man was able to restrain it.

However, there were also instances when they were not so popular. In October, 1862, they were locked overnight inside the store of Messrs. Rosenfeldt, stationer, and Collins, jeweler, probably to help rid the premises of rats. So incensed were they at being denied their freedom that during the night they ran wild through the store, smashing glass cases and littering the contents all over the place. On another occasion Lazarus was locked alone in the same store. Chafing against his confinement, he dashed his head against the thick plate glass, cracking it in several places, then jumped on the cases, and smashed up various delicate and valuable articles with perfect recklessness.

When Bummer arrived he could not get in, and Lazarus could not get out. Yet the two still settled down for the night together— one in the window display and the other on the sidewalk outside.

By this time they were truly established as characters of San Francisco and, on the night of October 22, 1862, they appeared on the stage of the Metropolitan Theatre as themselves in a burletta entitled "Life in San Francisco."

One day someone made a tragic mistake. He gave Bummer to a farmer in Alameda, suggesting that he would be an excellent sheep dog. However, Bummer immediately considered the sheep merely another form of rodent, and he went about attacking half a dozen of them before anyone realized what was happening.

Lazarus died in October, 1863, after eating some poisoned food. In its lengthy "Lament for Lazarus," the *Bulletin* suggested that the poisoner may have been the father of a boy who had accused the dog of biting him. Nevertheless, a $50 reward was offered for the identity of whoever did it, but was not publicly claimed. His hide was stuffed by a taxidermist and displayed in one of the many saloons around Montgomery and Clay streets.

> Bright dogs can never die! Lazarus sits in state, looking more natural than he did in life. His appointments are better. Formerly he had to lie on the pavement, now he reposes on a piece of velvet carpeting. Poets are served in the same way. They live in garrets till they die, and then they are put into Westminster Abbey.

Bummer lived another two years, although stories of him appeared with less frequency. He was inconsolable following the loss of his friend, and he rarely wandered far from the spot where Lazarus died. Three months later he was seen in the company of another dog who was dubbed Lazarus, Jr. A few months after that Samuel Clemens, who was visiting from Nevada and working as a local reporter on the *Call,* wrote that he had seen him with "a vagrant black puppy." But these appear to be brief encounters. For the most part he spent those last two years sad and lonely.

Sometime in August, 1865, a drunk kicked him down a stairway on Montgomery Street. Rumors circulated that he had died, but these were soon contradicted by reports that he was still very much alive. However, his body began to swell, and walking seemed to cause him great agony. He was accused of playing for sympathy, for he would often wait until a crowd gathered around offering him food before standing up and walking away, his head and tail erect. In retrospect, however, it seems he was proving his determination not to allow the agony to overpower him: he was fighting Death as resolutely as he had fought rats in earlier times.

On Sunday, October 8, 1865, San Francisco experienced its worst earthquake in living memory. After-shocks were felt throughout the next two weeks. Although nobody was killed, several of the older buildings were damaged beyond repair. Edward Jump illustrated the event in his usual jovial style in a lithograph entitled "Earth Quakey Times." There was a woman floating through the air with skirt billowing about her; a man appeared to be leaping from a roof; another man dashed into the street with only a towel draped around him; the street railway car lurched off its rails; men, women and children rushed about, while buildings tottered and tumbled upon them. Down the center of the road dashed Bummer, looking healthy and youthful, though leaning to one side. Several of the incidents depicted actually happened, according to lengthy reports in the *Alta.* Nevertheless, it is doubtful that Bummer was as healthy then as he seemed in the caricature. Despite his courageous battle against pain, his condition worsened, and it became increasingly difficult to tell just how near to death he was.

A month later he was carried off to a ranch in Hayes' Valley with the hope he might recover. But he died within a few hours.

Whereas the *Alta* and the *Bulletin* had been the only newspapers to devote much space to the dogs on a regular basis, once Bummer lay dying several others brought their readers up to date on the event. The result is a series of humorous eulogies and notices—some conflicting. One evening paper printed a sentimental description of how he died and then the following night had to admit that the dog still lived. There were at least a dozen newspapers in the town then, and competition was fierce. Several used the occasion as another arena in which they could lambaste each other.

Jump designed another of his caricatures in the form of a letter sheet, entitled "Bummer and Lazarus, The Damon and Pythias of San Francisco," to which was attached a satirical poem by "Trem." Another artist, S.Nooks, Jr., depicted the body of Bummer lying in state, surrounded by a gathering of local characters and

13

VIPs, while hovering above are the winged images of the two dogs reunited.

Several saloons in the neighborhood competed for the dead body in the belief that to have it stuffed and on display would be worth "one thousand dollars a year in any place of public resort." Even such august and diverse groups as The Academy of Natural Sciences, the Society of California Pioneers, The New Mining Bureau, the YMCA, and "two sensation preachers" were said to be interested.

An obituary by Samuel Clemens appeared in the Virginia City *Territorial Enterprise,* and was later reprinted in the magazine *Californian.* Rather than fall in line with the laudatory approach adopted by the San Francisco writers, he chose to suggest that it was about time Bummer died anyway. He did not link the death with the savage kick three months earlier, but instead pronounced the cause of death to be natural—"full of years, and honor, and disease, and fleas."

In retrospect it is amusing to note how he had underestimated the impact these two dogs had had on San Francisco, especially when we recall this *non sequitur* at the end of his 1865 obituary:

> In fact, Bummer should have died sooner; there was a time when his death would have left a lasting legacy of fame to his name. Now, however, he will be forgotten in a few days.

THE NEWSPAPERS. . .

In order to retain the original flavor of these nineteenth century newspaper accounts, no attempt has been made to standardize their idiosyncratic spelling and punctuation, nor to tamper with the inconsistencies to be found within some of the reports.

Courtesy: The Bancroft Library, University of California

16

Daily Alta California.

SUNDAY, FEBRUARY 4, 1860

MONTGOMERY STREET, SAN FRANCISCO FASHIONABLE HEADQUARTERS.—The great headquarters of bustle, excitement and fashion of San Francisco is Montgomery street. Truly, it presents a picture unequalled in its various phases, in California. Montgomery street is the grand artery through which the tide of life delights to circulate. Here may be seen the costly equipages of the rich, and the humble rag-picker's cart, rolling side by side, each with its occupants equally intent upon the pleasure or business which has brought them out. Here the millionaire of the Pacific jostles the poor dinnerless stranger—the one with serious face calculating the chances of his latest investment, the other eyeing with greedy looks the tempting contents of the restaurant windows. Omnibuses, express wagons, fast nags and jaded hacks rattle and bang over the pavement, and keep up a roar which betokens the immense amount of business transacted in this thoroughfare. The costumes of many nations are seen there; the language of all are spoken. All the noises, cries and other evidences of a metropolitan place are heard in Montgomery street. The voices of the news-boys crying the *Extra Alta,* are those of New York; the dress of the dandyish group who slap their neatly polished boots with their canes on the opposite corner, has nothing provincial in it. The hurried step of the business man, and the merchant's clerk, smacks of city and its clock-like regularity of motion. The crowd have that jostling gait only seen in great cities. The signs over the doors and the innumerable dodges of advertising are all those of a city, with a distinct character about them, serving as models for all others to imitate. Look at the streams of elegantly dressed ladies, who float dreamily along the spacious sidewalks. Observe the taste displayed in their dress—the unmistakable air of metropolitan superiority with which they enter the splendid shops; how daintily they step in and out of their carriages. And the shops! Glance inside if you dare face the battery of loveliness there congregated, and mark the unsurpassed display of rich goods; hear the rustling of silks and satins—the far-fetched products of foreign lands wafted from the Indies, China, or Europe into the lap of San Francisco; the delicate fabrics of the loom—observe all this, and a thousand other evidences of San Francisco's wealth, and then deny it who can, that in Montgomery street, all this centres, and from it radiates and affects the whole gay and business life of the State. Ay, indeed! good old Montgomery street! We cherish it with the sentiment of a first love—all the way from Washington street to Tucker's new building [between Pine and California streets]—both sides—and fearlessly challenge any one to deny it, the supreme position in the world of fashion and elegance, that we have accorded it. And then, at night, how everybody after dinner crowds into Montgomery street, and saunters lazily along "filled with distressful bread," looking in at the great plate glass windows resplendent with gold and silver and precious jewels. What a sweeping along of dainty dresses and "loves of bonnets," and what a mild radiance and smell of frangipani and musk fills all the air! all crowding to visit the gaieties of the season where sweet strains of music strike the ear, or crowded audiences make the theatres resound with laughter and applause. There is an atmosphere about Montgomery street and three or four of the tributary arteries which conduct into it to swell its ever surging tide which is decidedly redolent of a great capital city—and all this combines to tell of the wealth and progress of San Francisco in its commerce, in its population, in its artistical taste and disposition. The time must come however as the city increases in population when the glory of Montgomery street will depart. It will be useless to try and enter within its limited space the vast trade in costly goods which San Francisco's two hundred thousand inhabitants will require in 1870. By that time the demands of wholesale commerce will have encroached upon it with the inexorable certainty that has created revolutions in other streets within the last five years, and probably Market street—which will then have become completely built up, and one of the finest thoroughfares in America—will be the Broadway of San Francisco.

Daily Alta California.

SATURDAY, APRIL 21, 1860

THE DOG NUISANCE—STRYCHNINE NEEDED.— The city is infested with thousands of worthless mangy curs of dogs, whose numbers have at last become intolerable. We never knew a city in America so cursed with the canine nuisance as San Francisco. By night, and by day, they haunt the streets — yelping and snarling, flying at horsemen, and barking at whoever moves by them on a fast walk. Ladies have been frequently attacked, and we can recall many instances where little children have been dangerously torn by them.... There are really about three times as many dogs in this city as the place can support, and how they all live we never could surmise. Sometimes at night their howling is enough to drive one distracted, and it would seem that if they rest in the daytime, it is the better to exert their pectoral organs after dark.... The worst of the evil is that the accursed beasts increase and multiply like rats, and at this rate, the city will soon be overrun with them. We call on the proper authorities to enforce the law against dogs, and rid us of this crying nuisance. It is only due to the climate that hundreds of people are not every year destroyed by hydrophobia....

Daily Alta California.

FRIDAY, JANUARY 18, 1861

SAN FRANCISCO DOGS—"BUMMER" AND HIS PROTEGE.— One of the features of San Francisco is a specimen of the canine race—a black Newfoundland dog, known by the significant cognomen of "Bummer." Nobody is able to say, with certainty, who the animal belongs to, where he came from, or who was his master originally. All that is known is, that he made his appearance on the sidewalk of Montgomery street immediately after the death of his predecessor "Bruno," whose taking off by strychnine, about a year ago, was extensively commented upon by the press. "Bruno" was no less a bummer, i.e. "loafer," than his successor —but "peace to his mange," as was said at the time of his death. "Bummer" has the run of all the restaurants and lunch tables, and knows by instinct the hour of lunch. He is universally recognized, and manages to pick up a living by hook or by crook among his numerous friends. His beat is on the east side of Montgomery, between Washington and Sacramento streets. The dog actually knows every saloon on that entire beat. But he has shown another trait, within a few days, which does him no little credit. "Bummer" can take his own part, and, if needs be, take that of any poor acquaintance who may need assistance. Three or four days ago, a poor, lean, mangy cur was attacked in the street by a larger dog, and was getting unmercifully walloped, when "Bummer's" ire being aroused at the unequal contest, he rushed in and gave the attacking canine such a rough handling that he was glad to quit the field yelping, and making the best dog time on record. The poor cur had one of his legs half bitten through, and having limped upon the sidewalk, he proceeded to scrape an acquaintance with his deliverer, "Bummer," who thenceforth took him under his special protection. Every night since, that the "twa dogs" have slept coiled up together, close to some doorway—Bummer always giving the lame cur the inside berth, and trying to keep him as warm as possible. All day, yesterday, as Bummer walked deliberately up and down his beat, looking into people's faces to see if he could recognize an acquaintance or a lunch-eater, the cur limped to and fro with him, evidently placing the highest confidence in his companion's proceedings, and counting him as his friend and protector. Bummer seemed to feel the weight of the responsibility, and regarded his sorry looking protege with pity, not unmingled by contempt at his woe-begone appearance. The two were seen huddled up together in the most fraternal manner, last night after 12 o'clock.

Daily Alta California.

FRIDAY, APRIL 12, 1861

AN INSTANCE OF GROSS INGRATITUDE.—Everybody remembers the dog "Bummer," who has been wandering up and down Montgomery street for the last six months without a master or claimant. "Bummer" one day defended a poor, lame dog—a mangy cur named "Lazarus"—from the attack of a larger animal, and thenceforth the "two dogs" traveled in company—"Bummer" making him his protege, sleeping beside him on the sidewalks and protecting him from all assailants. This instance of canine fraternity was looked upon as quite remarkable, and the newspapers quoted it as an illustration of the generosity of brutes, whose sympathies were thus shown to be as acute as that of man. Well, the two dogs continued their brotherly feelings—keeping together and sharing each other's fortunes—"Bummer" always taking the best care of his miserable friend, and allowing him the lion's share of whatever turned up to eat, until "Lazarus," now cured of his lameness, became the likeliest-looking creature of the two. Last week some evil-minded person had the cruelty to shoot "Bummer," wounding his leg in such a manner that he could scarcely walk. The animal began to mope and slink about in obscure corners, as sick dogs generally do, upon which "Lazarus," forgetting the generosity of his benefactor, coolly deserted him, trotting off to hunt up more profitable acquaintances, and "Bummer" experiences the sting of ingratitude. That is, he may be supposed to experience it, for there is no question as to the chivalrous care which he took of his companion when their conditions were reversed. He might console himself, however, with the reflection that such instances are not confined to the canine race.

Daily Alta California.

THURSDAY, SEPTEMBER 12, 1861

THE STREET DOGS.—The inseparable canines known as "Bummer" and "Lazarus," about whom so much has been said and written, attracted an unusual crowd, on Montgomery street, yesterday. "Bummer," seeing another dog gnawing a bone, rushed to seize it. In the effort he proved unsuccessful, and was retreating, when "Lazarus" rushed to the rescue, and the two got possession of the coveted treasure, which they quietly picked by the curb stone, to the entertainment of the spectators.

Daily Alta California.

TUESDAY, APRIL 22, 1862

VAGRANT CURS.—The ordinance to prevent dogs running at large in the public streets has been passed to print, in the Board of Supervisors, which is tantamount to its final passage. Owners of valuable dogs will hereafter see to it that their canine property is not allowed to stray from their homes. It is tacitly understood amongst policemen, that the dogs "Bummer" and "Lazarus" are especially exempted from the provisions of this stringent ordinance. The order prohibits all dogs hereafter from running at large in any of the public streets, north of

Ninth and east of Larkin streets, without being properly muzzled. Any police officer may kill any dog found running unmuzzled or not lead by a string or chain. The Poundkeeper is authorized to take any dog to the public pound, and if not redeemed in forty-eight hours thereafter, he may be killed. The redeemer must pay the Pound Master $5. The Poundkeeper is entitled to receive for each and every dog taken by him the sum of 50 cents. If the above ordinance is strictly enforced, this city will be soon rid of the innumerable canine nuisances which have so long infested every street, highway and byway.

Daily Evening Bulletin.

THURSDAY, MAY 1, 1862

THE BEST LAW OF THE SEASON.—The supervisors have won more favor by their new Dog Ordinance than the Legislators by all their winter's work. The dog law is now in full force and effect, and unless dogs are muzzled, their owners need not be surprised to hear of their confinement in the pound, or death at the hands of the police. No executions have yet been made under the law, as it is the wish to give the owners of dogs ample time to procure their muzzles, and then all dogs—both great and small, good, bad and indifferent—will have to share the common fate. The boys will do a good business too, in catching dogs and delivering them to the poundkeeper, at four bits a head. A small fortune might be made in that line on Pacific street, and indeed in any other street of the city. All persons having valuable dogs had better attend to the matter at once if they wish to save them. Moreover, those who keep a houseful of dogs which they are too tenderhearted to kill, and which water will not drown, will know how to get rid of them. Take them out on a morning walk. The boys that capture them will make money, and the poundkeeper will be thankful for the lengthened list of subjects.

Daily Evening Bulletin.

ENFORCING THE DOG-LAW.—The new dog ordinance is now being rigidly enforced, and all dogs unmuzzled will be summarily dealt with. Over 50 were captured yesterday and taken to the pound, out of which some three or four of the ugliest curs among them were released upon the payment of $5 by the owners. The owners generally complain that their animals were arrested just as they happened to run out of doors for a breath of air. One poor woman went to the pound today to "bail out" her pet. She had but $2 in the world, and that she wished to pay for her dog's freedom. The pound keeper had no power to reduce the bail in her case, and sent her to the Mayor. What success she met with there is not yet known. Tomorrow afternoon a general slaughter of the "unredeemed" will take place. The neighbors in the vicinity of the pound were serenaded all last night with a 50 dog chorus.

Daily Evening Bulletin.

THE DOG WAR.—The Poundkeeper has to-day 47 dogs in bond, waiting to be either redeemed or slaughtered. The duties of the office have become so onerous that he has been obliged to employ an "executioner," to do the "heavy business" of the office. The Poundkeeper makes the arrests, and keeps the records, while the executioner takes the unredeemed to some dark and lonely spot, and despatches his victims. They are then buried without ceremony or pomp—the dainty poodle and the mangy cur, the bristling terrier and the sleek spaniel, all lie in one common grave, and are soon forgotten.

Daily Evening Bulletin.

WEDNESDAY, JUNE 11, 1862

CUR NON?

A GROWL FROM THE POUND

You suffer the dog of high degree
Unmolested abroad to be;
The spaniel sleek and the glossy hound
Are never housed in the public pound.

Cur Non?

But the mangy slut and her starving pup
That would scour your streets and clean
  them up
Are not allowed to repose their bones
Undisturbed on the paving stones.

Cur Non?

Say, city fathers, why will you not give
To us as to them the right to live?
To us as well as the battened hound
The right to exist outside the pound?

Cur Non?

I ask in vain—you do not reply.
Then list to me and I'll tell you why:
Because we were what you would be,
A young republic—entirely free.

Cur Non?

We followed no master's whistle or beck,
We wore no collar about the neck;
And even now would death prefer
To the muzzle that saves your pampered cur.

Cur Non?

BUMMER.

San Francisco, June 11, 1862.

Daily Alta California.

SATURDAY, JUNE 14, 1862

THE CANINE VAGRANTS.—It was hoped that the dogslayer would spare the life of the poor vagrant dog known as "Lazarus," the inseparable companion of another canine brute, "Bummer" by name, and that from and after the passage of the dog ordinance, both would be considered as exempted from the provisions of this law. The former was impounded a day or two ago, but released through the exertions of his human friends, for yesterday we observed the four-legged Damon and Pythias stretched out together on the sidewalk, away up Washington street, and snoozing cosily under the hot rays of the noonday sun.

Daily Alta California.

MONDAY, JUNE 16, 1862

A SYMPATHETIC COMMUNITY.—Several hundreds of signatures have been obtained to petitions praying that the dogs "Bummer" and "Lazarus" be exempted from the provisions of the canine murder order. These will be presented to the Board of Supervisors this evening, and there is no reason to doubt their granting them immunity from this act.

Daily Evening Bulletin.

TUESDAY, JUNE 17, 1862

BOARD OF SUPERVISORS. — The Board of Supervisors met last evening at the usual hour, Mr De la Montanya being the only member absent — the Mayor presiding.

THE "BUMMER" AND "LAZARUS" PETITION

The Mayor announced a petition in regard to the noted dogs — *Bummer* and *Lazarus* — received and placed on file. It runs thus — being very numerously signed:

To the Honorable Mayor and Board of Supervisors of the City and County of San Francisco. — Your petitioners respectfully represent that they are law-abiding citizens of said city and county, and entertain due respect for the orders of your Honorable Body. Your petitioners especially approve of an acquiesce in the "Dog Law" intended to purge the city of the "mongrel, whelp and curs of low degree," which have become such a nuisance. But as general laws have exceptions, your petitioners beg leave to urge upon your Honors to recognize two exceptions to the operation of this most useful enactment. Your petitioners think they can show such grounds of exception as will warrant the interference for which they pray. To do this properly, however, it is necessary to give a brief history of the two for whom this exemption is sought. The elder and most energetic is designated by a name, which, if not euphonius, is expressive — *Bummer* — well known to most of the constituents of your Honors. He is of Scotch origin and of respectable parentage, but from the consequences of certain youthful indiscretions, far removed from the sympathy of his early friends and protectors. Whatever may have been his faults, however, they are fully atoned for by his fidelity, gratitude and unflinching courage. His companion is known by a name obtained from a rare work, with which your Honors are not probably acquainted. The origin of *Lazarus* is wrapt in darkness. His chief excellence consists in the facility with which he can destroy rats, and as these animals infest the various departments, it is a quality which gives him a peculiar value to the public. But your petitioners rely especially upon the general affection felt for these two animals, on account of the lessons of protection and faithful association their union has daily presented for two years past— and in all earnestness pray the consecration of the two dogs as city property, whereby they may be exempted from taxation or destruction, and suffered, as heretofore, to wander unmolested in pursuit of their daily food. They are harmless, and their union and the circumstances which led to it, which are so generally known as to require no repetition, fully authorize the special protection which is asked in their behalf. And, as in duty bound, your petitioners will ever pray.

Daily Alta California.

TUESDAY, JUNE 17, 1862

CITY CURS.—A mammoth petition was presented to the Board of Supervisors, last evening, praying that the public dogs, "Bummer" and "Lazarus," be exempt from the provisions of the present stringent Ordinance for the destruction of the race. The Board received and referred the petition. The Poundkeeper, during the last week, impounded 104 curs, of which 90 were slaughtered and 14 redeemed. The amount of cash received was $70.

UPARALLELED SAGACITY.—Whether the dogs "Bummer" and "Lazarus" were aware or not of the fact that a memorial was to be presented for their relief last evening, certain it is that at the hour of convening the Board of Supervisors they lay crouched at the threshold of the chamber, apparently eager to hear what was to be said and done for their benefit. If any man carried them there, it was a cute dodge to get favorable action on their petition; if they went there voluntarily, they ought to have free run of the town during the rest of their lives.

Daily Alta California.

TUESDAY, JUNE 24, 1862

DOGS STOPPING A RUNAWAY TEAM.—Yesterday afternoon, the notorious curs, "Bummer" and "Lazarus," chased a runaway team up Clay street, one taking one side of the thoroughfare, and one the other. On reaching the corner of Kearny, "Bummer" rushed in front of the horse and held him at bay until a man came up and caught the team, "Lazarus" being on hand to check any further advance. These dogs may now be considered in the employ of the city, and of course are exempt from taxation.

Daily Alta California.

FRIDAY, OCTOBER 3, 1862

CANINE BURGLARS.—A new chapter is to be added to the history of the renowned dogs, "Bummer" and "Lazarus." On Tuesday night they entered the shop occupied by Messrs. Rosenfeldt, stationer, and Collins, jeweler, and quietly ensconcing themselves behind the counter, went to sleep, "perhaps to dream." At all events they were locked in for the night. Early yesterday morning a person passing heard a tremendous hubbub inside, and naturally suspecting burglars within, invoked the aid of sundry law-abiding citizens. Preparations were quietly made for capturing the rascals. The door was silently opened, when, on the instant, the inseparable canines rushed out. So sudden was the exit that the force scattered. On regaining their composure, the establishment was entered. It was at once discovered that the canines, chafing at their confinement, had jumped through glass cases, and otherwise done considerable damage. The most remarkable part of the story is, that from the moment of their unceremonious "clearing" up to a late hour last night they had not been seen in their usual haunts on the street. Doubtless, they fear "arrest" by the police!

Daily Evening Bulletin.

WEDNESDAY, OCTOBER 22, 1862

[In the "Amusements" column we find this announcement.]

METROPOLITAN THEATRE.—The dramas of *The Foundling of the Forest* and *Life in San Francisco* will be given this evening. Mrs. Hayne will appear in the former piece, and *Bummer* and *Lazarus* in the latter.

30

Daily Alta California.

TUESDAY, FEBRUARY 17, 1863

CANINE MARKET VISITORS.—The inseparable curs, "Bummer" and "Lazarus," have been in the habit lately of regularly visiting Washington Market at a certain hour in the morning, for their breakfast. They know precisely the stalls to go to for a sure meal, and never fail of getting their full before returning to their accustomed beat on Montgomery street.

Daily Alta California.

MONDAY, JULY 13, 1863

DAMAGES BY A CITY GUEST.—The canine paupers, Bummer and Lazarus, having been granted the freedom of the town by our City Fathers, the latter of course are responsible for their good behavior, and liable for their misdeeds. Lazarus got locked in Rosenfeld's Stationery Store, on Montgomery street, yesterday, having hid himself to get a good "snooze." Towards night he found himself in secure quarters. He tried to break jail, but it was no go. He dashed his head against the thick plate glass, cracking it in several places, then jumped on the cases, and smashed up various delicate and valuable articles with perfect recklessness. Bummer came along, but could give him no aid, and at midnight Lazarus occupied the show window bench, whilst his brother kept watch outside. The town may have a nice little bill of damages for these canine pranks!

32

Daily Evening Bulletin.

SATURDAY, OCTOBER 3, 1863

LAMENT FOR LAZARUS.

Lazarus is dead. He began to swell up in the course of the night, and passed gently away before the hour that Bummer has generally given him a rat for his morning meal. These two were very famous dogs. Their early history is like that of Rome mixed with much fable. Lazarus was certainly the senior dog of the two—some say he was very near, if not quite the pioneer dog of the town, while Bummer was little heard of until about Vigilance Committee times. Either alone might never have been worthy of an item—together, they were an institution like the Consolidation Act, or the Emperor Norton, whom everybody knew. Their portraits are in the windows. Their *cartes de visite* are in all well regulated albums. They had traits not laid down in Mayhew. Dogs generally are selfish—every one for himself. But Bummer and Lazarus shared their bones and flesh. In their social relations they shamed mankind and made the authors of our Divorce law blush as they passed. In repose, Bummer lay on the pavement asleep but showing his teeth notwithstanding; Lazarus lay half a length behind him, his head pillowed on Bummer's side fearless of mishaps, clearly confident that no harm could visit him while Bummer was his friend. In a fight Bummer always took the lead while Lazarus lay back and encouraged him. Bummer did the biting, Lazarus the barking. Bummer's forte was in his teeth, Lazarus' forte was in his tail which wagged fearfully when his friend was in the thick of the encounter. In case of a reverse, which, though rare, has happened before now Lazarus discovered a little the most genius. He was smart on a retreat, while Bummer never seemed to know that he was beaten but kept on showing his teeth till the victor was out of sight.

Their treatment of other dogs was not perhaps what it should be. Bummer was quite too

33

contemptuous—not even saluting one twice his size with any grace, while Lazarus would have fraternized with every mongrel in town if Bummer's head were turned. Like other best friends their natural dispositions differed. Lazarus prefered early morning walks—it was safer; Bummer was around evenings—it paid best.

Other dogs live to eat, and fawn upon their masters; Bummer and Lazarus lived to exterminate rats. Lazarus had no master but Bummer; while Bummer was an orphan and never had a master. In front of the Clay street French market we have seen two or three men for a day's sport tear up the sidewalk and begin to shovel out live rats. Though the men worked faithfully and threw out rats, two to the spade, not one of them could strike the ground without meeting Bummer's fierce teeth half way. Then it was fearful to see Lazarus shake the poor, broken-necked creatures. Occasionally, Bummer would fall back and wait for Lazarus to go in, and then it was delightful to see how his bushy tail was affected with joy of his weak friend's enterprise. Between the two, no rat

ever saw the light of their eyes and escaped alive.

Their pedigree is not on record. Lazarus was supposed to be a cross between a cur and a hound, with a dash of the terrier that was not developed until he went into partnership. In color he was of a yellowish black—and proudest of the black. Bummer was bull in his fighting quarters and Newfoundland in his vital parts. For color he was pure white and pure black, spotted. Two drunken fellows quarreled as to his color one day. One bet he was white and proved it by showing the white, the other bet he was black and said any fool could see it. Bummer was an honest dog—Lazarus a faithful one.

Lazarus was sly like Major Bagstock. Close observers say that when there was a fat bone which he could snatch unobserved, he was ingenious about getting it in possession. On such occasions he seemed suddenly fond of solitude, and when half an hour later he returned, fetching the bone to share it with his partner, there was not any marrow in the place where the marrow ought to be. Bummer magnanimously pretended never to see these evidences of his friend's bad faith.

They loved rats—that is, they loved to kill them. The city is said to be full of rats, and that fact kept Bummer and Lazarus full—of employment. The town rings to-day with stories of their prowess in this line. Gould & Martin last April cleared off a gallery in their fruit market, and during the process the two dogs, with the aid of some clubs wielded by earnest men, killed over 400 rats! That is vouched for as a true story. At another place of business—not a restaurant—where an effort was on foot to get rid of the rats, Bummer and Lazarus killed 85 of the vermin in about 20 minutes. Nothing could stand before them. It is notable—and a moral might be drawn from it—their different ways of doing things. Both were death on rats, and they shared alike the profits of their enterprise. Then why need Bummer always expose himself to the kicks and get the enmity of all rat-dom, while Lazarus could grow fat, and have never an enemy? But the tale of Lazarus was significant, too. It was Bummer that always showed his teeth, but Lazarus was charged yesterday with having bitten a boy, and it is thought that the boy's father threw the poison that made Lazarus in a night too fat to live! The dog that had no enemy dies by violence, while he who was the terror of all the rats on the coast, survives! The party that claimed to own Lazarus, because he bailed him out of the Pound once and got the Supervisors to ease his case over with a special ordinance, has offered a reward of $50 for the discovery of the man who threw the poison. The brevity of this article is due to our consideration that the people read the newspapers and believe them, and we do not want to so prejudice the community that when the slayer of Lazarus is indicted it will be impossible to get a jury.

Both dogs loved their liberty and abhorred confinement. One Saturday night, Bummer got locked up in a news depot. Lazarus traveled Montgomery street, visited all his old haunts, hunted high and low, refused food, was disconsolate all Sunday. On Monday morning he did not even go to Chase's for his breakfast, but resumed his search. Passing the shop where Bummer lay solitary among the literature, he heard a scratching on the window. Instantly, Lazarus made a dive at the window, for it was his long lost brother. The plate glass was shivered to atoms, the friends were united, and together they strolled where the doors were opened, into the light of day. On another occasion, a party, either heedless, or thinking he would make rats thinner on his premises thereby, locked them both together in a jeweller's shop. There was a terrible scene in that party's premises next morning—valuables scattered, invaluables ruined! Nobody ever made the mistake of locking them inside again. They were the best friends of the community when independent and at liberty—worse than iconoclasts, when caged.

A curious mistake was once made as to the character of Bummer. A gentleman from the country, meeting a knight of the quill in town, made known his desire to get a good shepherd's dog. "Then I'm your man," said the knight, "here's Bummer, a splendid shepherd's dog." So Bummer went that day to Alameda, and was entrusted straightway with the care of a flock of sheep. Next morning some half a dozen fancy rams were lacerated carcasses. Bummer doubtless fancied them a higher style of rats, and treated them accordingly. In his proper life of freeing the city of rats he was unapproachable; but as you would not set Gilmore's Swamp Angel to belching Greek fire to illuminate a peaceful city, so it was possible even to put Bummer in the wrong place.

The taxidermists are busy stuffing Lazarus's skin to-day, and the newspaper men are writing their finest eulogies. In our feeble attempt we have perhaps glorified the living Bummer more than the departed Lazarus, gliding unwittingly into that course because we cannot help thinking that a live Bummer is better than a dead dog. Besides, the better part of Lazarus still lives—in his friend, without whom he would have been unworthy of an epitaph, his memory survives. Bummer is still around, and the rats lie low.

Daily Evening Bulletin.

MONDAY, OCTOBER 26, 1863

LAZARUS REDIVIVUS.

Lazarus has risen, and is stuffed. A skillful taxidermist has taken away from him all that was fleshy, and left of him only what is imperishable. Bright dogs can never die! Lazarus sits in state, looking more natural than he did in life. His appointments are better. Formerly he had to lie on the pavement, now he reposes on a piece of velvet carpeting. Poets are served in the same way. They live in garrets till they die, and then they are put into Westminster Abbey. The world that refused them meat gives them a monument—alive they asked for bread, dead and their countrymen give them a stone. In his new condition Lazarus looks bright and erect—and there is a vigilant expression in his eye, as though he smelt a rat. At the same time an expression lingers on his countenance, as though he had done something wrong in dying and getting stuffed before Bummer. It is the first time he ever took precedence of his companion, and probably will be the last. Poor Lazarus, he is mortified that he was not permitted to share his stuffing with Bummer, who always divided his bones with him. Nor is there any room for Bummer on the carpet. He has visions of his old friend and companion stretched out on stones while he himself is on velvet. Lovely in their lives, in their death the friends had to be divided. A jeremiad might be written, but where shall we look for a Tupper to gracefully perform the grateful duty. How the author of Proverbial Philosophy and other verbiage would have expanded with the theme. Given, two dogs with but a single bark, two tails that wagged as one, a death and a separation, and what might not a Tupper have done. The "Greeting to Alexandra" would have been no where beside the

Farewell to Lazarus. Would not his numbers have run something thus?

> 100,000 Pities,
> 100,000 Pities,
> And 100,000 more!
> O shining skin of Lazarus,
> Stuffed out to put upon the Plaza as
> No dog was stuffed before.
> Sleep on—let Bummer snore,
> And chase for rats the city o'er,
> But you'll not do it any more.
> 100,000 Pities,
> And 100,000 more.
> Let all the canines roar
> The dog-gone city o'er,
> And let the steeples chime it—
> 100,000 Pities,
> And 100,000 more.
> And let but Tupper rhyme it—
> Though Tupper is a bore—
> And sing from door to door,
> 100,000 Pities,
> And 100,000 more!

If the above is not what Martin Farquhar would have written, it is very certainly near it. And the honors and title which the Prince of Wales conferred on him for the Alexandrine verses would be as nothing to the decorations and emoluments which our Emperor would have showered on him—the freedom of the city and access to all free lunches about town, given under the Imperial hand and seal.

Lazarus in his present state was introduced to Bummer. Bummer evidently recognized him as his long lost brother, and commenced a search for the strawberry mark, but that had gone to seed. Bummer seemed to know that a wondrous change had come over his friend, and was puzzled to account for it. Not as of old did he arise and offer Bummer the softest plank to lie down upon, happy and content if he could only rest his head on Bummer's flank. Bummer saw there was a mystery and looked awe-struck. He may not have known that Lazarus was behind the curtain and familiar with problems that were blinding to him; he may not have known that whether rats were large or small, scarce or plenty, was all one to Lazarus now. But he certainly looked and acted as though he were impressed, and wandered away with a softer expression about his grim nether jaw than it had known for many long years.

The name of the taxidermist who has given Lazarus to immortality is E. F. Lorquin. The task is well done, and at a cost of about $50. F. Martin, whom Lazarus was wont to follow before breakfast and obey before dinner in life, has been the prime mover in the matter and footer of the bill. But for the body of Lazarus there are many claimants. The Pioneers want it, and the Supervisors are likely to make overtures. But these latter would probably serve the dog as they served the aerolite a few years ago. To no one individual or association should the honor of keeping the remains be entrusted— pass them around.

Daily Alta California,

TUESDAY, OCTOBER 27, 1863

"AS NATURAL AS LIFE."—Some skillful taxidermist has made the dead dog "Lazarus" look as natural as new. The skin has been very admirably stuffed. So natural does the canine appear that "Bummer," the surviving companion of the deceased, gave positive evidence by his manner that he believed "Lazarus" had been only sleeping.

Daily Alta California.

FORMED A NEW PARTNERSHIP.—"Bummer" having worn the weeds of mourning for the usual period, and having arrived at the time when Fashion permits her votaries to become genteelly consolable, and commence looking for a new comforter, has given the memory of his late lamented friend and fellow-traveler the shake; he has formed a new partnership, and is now going from place to place holding ratification meetings in honor of the event. The new partner in the firm—Lazarus, Jr.—is a likely looking bull pup, not yet arrived to full size and age of usefulness, but bids fair to eventually rival his great namesake and predecessor in activity and affection for the senior partner in the concern.

Daily Morning Call.

ANOTHER LAZARUS.—The lamented Lazarus departed this life about a year ago, and from that time until recently poor Bummer has mourned the loss of his faithful friend in solitude, scorning the sympathy and companionship of his race with that stately reserve and exclusiveness which has always distinguished him since he became a citizen of San Francisco. But, for several weeks past, we have observed a vagrant black puppy has taken up with him, and attends him in his promenades, bums with him at the restaurants, and watches over his slumbers as unremittingly as did the sainted Lazarus of other days. Whether that puppy really feels an unselfish affection for Bummer, or whether he is actuated by unworthy motives, and goes with him merely to ring in on the eating houses through his popularity at such establishments, or whether he is one of those fawning sycophants that fasten upon the world's heroes in order that they may be glorified by the reflected light of greatness, we cannot yet determine. We only know that he hangs around Bummer, and snarls at intruders upon his repose, and looks proud and happy when the old dog condescends to notice him. He ventures upon no puppyish levity in the presence of his prince, and essays no unbecoming familiarity, but in all respects conducts himself with the respectful decorum which such a puppy so situated should display. Consequently, in time, he may grow into high favor.

Edgar M. Branch, Editor of "Clemens of the 'Call'" (University of California Press, 1969), gives credit for this report to Samuel Clemens.

Daily Alta California.

SUNDAY, FEBRUARY 28, 1864

COURT PROCEEDINGS.
Saturday, February 27th.
County Court.—Cowles J.
AN ARTIST'S WORK—PROFILE OF A FAVORITE DOG. Rouse & Jump vs. Turner Cowing—This is a case which has for some time been the subject of litigation. It was tried once before by this Court. The plaintiffs, Rouse & Jump, are artists, and the action brought was for the recovery of the sum of $65 for twenty-five large lithographic pictures of the defendant and his dog in hunting costume, which the defendant refused to pay for on the ground, as he alleged, that the picture was not a faithful likeness of himself and his dog. The dog was represented as being a favorite of the defendant and it was also stated as a grave objection to the picture that the mouth of the dog, as given in the picture, was too large to suit the defendant's

idea of symmetry of form of that portion of the animal's developments. The dog was also considered to be too "Lazarus" and "Bummer" like to suit the taste of admirers of well-bred quadrupeds of the favorite dog species. The costs in the case up to the present will amount to some hundreds of dollars. All the pictures taken were in Court, and there was even one of the two comic celebrities, "Bummer" and "Lazarus", gazing longingly on the redoubtable Emperor Norton, while luxuriating in the sweet things to be had and obtained at a "free lunch" bar. This picture was also the work of Rouse & Jump, of whom it was admitted that in the execution of it they had manifested a more than ordinary amount of artistic skill. The case was tried before a jury, who found for the plaintiffs a verdict for the full amount claimed, with the costs of suit.

Mr. Cook and Mr. Hittell appeared for the defendant.

Daily Evening Bulletin.

THURSDAY, AUGUST 25, 1864

[The following is buried in a lengthy report on the opening of The Ladies' Christian Commission Fair at Union Hall—which was intended as a fund-raiser for troops wounded in the Civil War.]

The most satisfactory sights to many were in the art gallery and museum....On the walls are hung a variety of ancient and curious objects—an autograph letter of George Washington; a sword which was used by a gallant Yankee in the Revolution; a hat worn by the rebel Gen. Stuart; autographs of Stonewall Jackson and other rebel leaders; a shot-pouch that once belonged to Kit Carson; old manuscripts of various sorts, and articles of Indian manufacture. The skin of the dog Lazarus is there, stuffed by the taxidermist's skill to such a life-like look that it would drive Bummer and Montgomery street wild with joy. A number of other stuffed animals occupy cases near by, and the room is well filled with a variety of curious articles....

Daily Alta California.

THURSDAY, SEPTEMBER 14, 1865

"BUMMER" IN A BAD WAY. — Some weeks since a drunken bummer, who ought at least to roast in a place as hot as the Upper Sacramento Valley for the term of his natural life, or longer, kicked poor old "Bummer" down a stairway on Montgomery street and injured him so that he has never recovered and is not likely ever to recover. His body is now swollen to twice its usual size, and the poor old fellow appears to be at death's door.

Daily Evening Bulletin.

FRIDAY, SEPTEMBER 15, 1865

NOT DEAD YET. — Reports have been in circulation for a week past that our universally known and highly esteemed citizen "Bummer" was on his last legs — that he was, in fact, dying the death of a dog in the public streets, and the places that know him now would soon know him no more forever. We are happy to be able to state that there is no truth in the reports. Bummer received a kick the other day from some uncivilized fellow bummer who was envious of his good name, and he has suffered somewhat from the belly-ache ever since; but as for dying, he never thought of the thing, although he has a fondness for death's twin sister, sleep. Sympathizing friends who gather around him as he lies dozing on the sidewalks, and imagine him in the agonies of death, may therefore dry their tears. This morning, while a party of mourners were standing around his prostrate body in Clay street, and lamenting his untimely end, Bummer suddenly jumped up and walked across the street with head and tail erect, looking as fresh and hearty as when he first arrived here in the "fall of '49 or spring of '50." The party were reluctantly forced to the conclusion that their old friend had become demoralized by bad associates, and had taken to practising that stale old trick of common bummers, called a "sell."

Courtesy: The Bancroft Library, University of California

44

Daily Alta California.

MONDAY, OCTOBER 9, 1865

THE GREAT SENSATION OF THE SEASON.

SAN FRANCISCO GETS A SHAKE-UP WHICH MAKES THINGS CRACK—GREAT EXCITEMENT, WHICH QUICKLY SUBSIDES—SOME DAMAGE DONE TO PROPERTY, BUT NO LIVES LOST, AND THE WHOLE TOWN MORE SCARED THAN HURT.

At precisely fifteen minutes to one P.M. yesterday, the city of San Francisco was visited by the heaviest earthquake shocks ever felt in this vicinity by "the oldest inhabitants." Heretofore our earthquakes have been trifling affairs, startling for the moment, but nowise serious in their results, and more a subject for joking and quizzing among friends and acquaintances than of serious anxiety to anybody. This demonstration was, however, of a more noteworthy character, and its effects were decidedly more startling and lasting.

. . .

The only accidents worthy of note, which came to our knowledge, were the following: Alexander Badger, Secretary of the San Francisco Olympic Club, was in the hall of the Club, on Sutter street, when the earthquake occurred, and fearing the fall of the building, sprang out of a side window to the roof of the Metropolitan Market. Unfortunately, he struck upon the skylight and went through to the main floor of the building, receiving injuries of so severe a character as to cause him extreme pain, and to a certain extent endanger his life. He was carried home by his friends, and will receive all possible care and attention.

. . .

Several of the bathers at the North Beach Sanitarium Bath House took to the street, habited in the severely classic costume in vogue in the Garden of Eden before the introduction of fig leaf aprons, creating a profound sensation among the outside barbarians.

. . .

On Bush street, a lady who was engaged in washing an infant of very tender age, ran screaming into the street. She stood on the sidewalk for some time swinging something in her hand, which at first was taken for a dressed chicken by the bystanders, but which began to speak for itself in language which placed it at once in the category of a different class of animated nature. She was holding it by the foot, head downwards, and had forgotten all about what she had in hand. . . .

Daily Morning Call.

WEDNESDAY, OCTOBER 11, 1865

JUMP AT IT AGAIN.—That prince of caricaturists, the mirth-provoking Jump, produced, yesterday morning, his second representation of "Quaky Times." [sic] The scenes he has depicted, if not as large as life, are more than twice as natural. In order to comprehend the entire history in a single representation, he has made locality conform to his purpose, and concentrated the city in a section of Howard street. The young lady jumping from a window on one side of the street has its parallel in the man throwing himself incontinently out of the Olympic window on the opposite side. Dr. Peck's congregation is adjourning en masse, and the Reverend Doctor adjourns conspicuously with them—the crowd blending with a rum-mill congregation which is adjourning on the opposite side of the street. The woman, with her naked infant dangling by the leg, is prominent in the foreground, and the buildings generally are doing the behest of a first-class earthquake. The picture is exhibited in Roos's window, Russ House Block.

Daily Morning Call.

THURSDAY, NOVEMBER 2, 1865

IN ARTICULO MORTIS.—At a late hour last evening, old "Bummer"—relict, we might say, of "Lazarus," and honored among dogs—whose remarkable sagacity has won for him a consideration rarely extended by men to his species, exhibited signs of approaching dissolution, and was conveyed on a dray, by a humane person, to a place where he might die in peace. For some time past, "Bummer" has given his legion of friends to understand that the place that knew him then would soon know him no longer, and he would in a short time be gathered unto "Lazarus." To communicate this fact he has employed almost human intelligence. Often would he attract a sympathizing crowd to witness the departure of his fleeting breath, and hear his last words, and all at once astonish them by getting up from his dying bed, with a solemn but determined air, as much as to say, "My friends, thus will you see me ere long, but I've not selected my last words yet." This habit of his at length got to be looked upon as a ruse to find out how much he was respected, or hear what kind of an epitaph he would be paraphrased in. Never since the demise of his affectionate companion, "Lazarus," has "Bummer" been completely himself. Occasionally he would call up the memories of the past, by making a raid on rats, but the subject was a painful one since his "Lazarus" was laid low, and latterly he has lived on his broad license to go where he pleased and get what he pleased. The consequence was, that he waxed fat with high living, and became unwieldy. But a short time ago, a mangy, distressed-looking cur attempted to fill the aching void occasioned by the loss of "Lazarus." "Bummer" merely endured his affectionate familiarities, and maintained a dignified reserve, which finally discouraged his new friend and he emigrated. To say that "Bummer" was a comely dog would be to falsify the record: ungainliness was stamped all over him. He had clumsiness in his gait, and anything but an enticing grin stereotyped on his countenance, keeping constantly before the people a set of teeth, like a law-abiding dog he was, not to be caught carrying concealed weapons. It was reported at a late hour last night that this remarkable animal had passed away. If he has, peace be to his bones; and every restaurant and butcher stand in the vicinity of Clay and Montgomery streets will attest that he had many. For months he has rarely permitted himself to go out of sight of the spot where his beloved "Lazarus" yielded up the vital principle—somewhere in the vicinity of Martin & Horton's—and here he had composed himself last evening for the closing scene of his career, when he was borne away by one who appreciated his merits, to die as a great dog should die. Benevolence was a prominent trait in "Bummer's" character, and the crowning act of his life was his kindness to poor "Lazarus," whom he found covered with sores and friendless; and "Lazarus" rewarded him with an undying affection.

"Large was his bounty, and his
    soul sincere,

Heaven did a recompense as largely send;
He gave to misery all he had—a tear—
He gained from Heaven—'t was all
    he asked—a friend."

From Thomas Gray's "Elegy Written in a Country Churchyard."

Daily Evening Bulletin.

FRIDAY, NOVEMBER 3, 1865

EXIT "BUMMER." The old canine celebrity of San Francisco, surnamed *Bummer*, long petted and beloved by her citizens, is dead. It is generally known that he has been on the decline for some weeks past, and many a lesson of *memento mori* has he taught to his fellow bummers who gathered around his prostrate form as he lay on the sidewalk on Clay street, gasping for breath and apparently in the last agonies. These deceptive appearances had been so often followed by a sudden revival of animation and apparent health in the poor dog that many came to regard them as theatrical tricks ignobly resorted to by old *Bummer* in his second childhood, to test the public sympathy and see whether he had not outlived his popularity as well as his usefulness. But those who did him the grievous injustice of such an insinuation will now see their error. *Bummer* was not a dog to resort to tricks at any period of his life, or for any purpose. He died as he lived, open and above board, *Bummer* by name, bummer by nature, no more, no less. It was evident to those who saw him on the sidewalk this afternoon that the period of his dissolution was fast approaching: and so it proved. As the shades of evening gathered around his eyelids, and "night drew her sable curtain down and pinned it with a star," (the dog star,) *Bummer* grew rapidly worse, and at 3 o'clock this morning yielded up the ghost without a murmur or a bark. Of the early history of *Bummer,* as of many famous characters that have figured in the world's history, little is known. He is said to have been born on the Western prairies, and in the days of his puppyhood he no doubt sported upon the green grass, and wagged his tail in happy innocence, and mingled his infantile bark with the laughter of his master's children. He made the journey to California across the plains, fought with the Indians, lost his master, became demoralized, and arrived in Sacramento a disappointed and disgusted dog. The disgust was not lessoned by a residence in that one horse town, and after a brief sojourn there he made his way to San Francisco where he found for the first time the true field for his genius and set to work to fulfil his mission. He at once quartered himself on the town, refusing to acknowledge any master but the City Fathers, and became rat killer to the corporation and public bummer. His independence and the novelty of his genius took with the people, and from that day he has been the pet of everybody, "without distinction of party." He has figured in all the sketches and caricatures of San Francisco life as prominently as other town celebrities, and the announcement of his demise will call up memories and associations in the minds of San Franciscans, now travelling in distant lands, quite as vivid as would be produced by more important events. His remarkable friendship for the insignificant dog *Lazarus* (since his ascension known as *Alta Lazarus*) will now doubtless meet its reward, and the twain can once more walk side by side, the chief lazzarone of the canine heaven.

P.S.—Since the above was printed in our second edition of yesterday we are informed that Bummer still survives, but is so near unto death that he is not likely to recover sufficiently to correct any errors in the above obituary, so we will let it pass.

THE DAILY EXAMINER.

FRIDAY, NOVEMBER 3, 1865

NOT DEAD, BUT GONE TO A RANCH.—The enterprising locals of the *Call* and *Bulletin* have murdered "Bummer" with malice aforethought in the columns of their respective columns. [sic] Now be it known the "Bum" is not dead, but has gone to a ranch to recruit. [sic]

Daily Dramatic Chronicle.

FRIDAY, NOVEMBER 3, 1865

"BUMMER" NOT DEAD!

The *Call* of this morning threw the whole community into an agony of anxiety and uncertainty by a constructive intimation that old "Bummer"—"Bummer" the quondam comrade of "Lazarus"—"Bummer" the Pride of the Village—was dead! Be easy, citizens—calm yourselves, calm yourselves; there is no truth in the item; it was only a smoothly-written sensation paragraph. "Bummer" has "gone to rusticate at Bessy's ranch, Hayes Valley," as a great placard at Martin & Horton's sets forth to the sighing crowds that hurry down to inquire about him.

Daily Morning Call.

SATURDAY, NOVEMBER 4, 1865

WHEN "BUMMER" DIED.—Notwithstanding a fellow-feeling has made the reporters of a morning and an evening paper cling to the hope that "Bummer" was one of "the few immortal dogs that were not born to die," yet he did die, and went the way of all dogs. He expired at Bessey's place, near Hayes' Park, at four o'clock Thursday afternoon. His skin has been whipped off, and will be stuffed by a taxidermist, after which it will be placed for exhibition at a well-known saloon. In the last characteristic act of "Bummer's" usefulness, is a striking instance of the ruling passion strong in death; the night before he died he "ratified the will divine—the faithful fixed the irrevocable sign that sealed his last suit," etc.—by killing a huge rodent, the corpse of which lay prone, on the following morning, alongside of the dying foe of his race.

THE DAILY EXAMINER.

SATURDAY, NOVEMBER 4, 1865

DEAD INDEED!—There is no longer any use of withholding from the public the appalling fact that "Bummer" is dead! He passed in his checks at 4 o'clock Thursday afternoon at the residence of Mr. Bessey, a Good Samaritan living near Hayes' Park, who took him out there hoping that a change of air might reinvigorate him. But the change was productive of no good, for Death had his grip upon old "Bummer," and no earthly power could "wake him to glory again."

Daily Alta California.

SUNDAY, NOVEMBER 5, 1865

BUMMER IS DEAD!—The ancient Bummer's death was posted on the canine *Bulletin* board some days since, but we hesitated to accept the mournful tidings as correct on such doubtful authority. Later and more reliable information confirms the report, however, and we tearfully give place to the following:

ELEGY ON BUMMER

BY A. BOHEMIAN, ESQ.

He, who was faithful to the end,
  The noble Bummer sleeps;
Gone hence to join his better friend,
  Where doggy never weeps.

All tears are wiped from Bummer's eyes,
  Good angels give him place;
E'en at the gates of Paradise,
  Barking glad notes of grace.

When Lazarus was ill, in need,
  'Twas Bummer bro't him bread;
Then brethren all, I pray take heed,
  To gain such praise when dead.

Ben Adhem's angel, in his log,
  Writes first who love their fellow men;
Be careful he don't place a dog
  Where he should place you, with his pen.

The Golden Era.

SUNDAY, NOVEMBER 5, 1865

BUMMER.

The health of no individual in this city has excited more attention in the public mind than that of the celebrated dog "Bummer." He occupied a space in the daily papers which many a biped would be glad to secure. The bulletin boards have abounded with notices to the effect that "Bummer is not dead, as reported," and that "Bummer had been taken to Bessey's ranch in Hayes' Valley to recuperate." May he never leave those classic shades. Fortunate Bummer! Lots of up country politicians would be glad to secure the fame which now belongs to Bummer.

BUMMERIANA. — DOG-MATIC SPIRIT OF THE PRESS.

EXIT "BUMMER." — The old canine celebrity of San Francisco, surnamed *Bummer*, long petted and beloved by her citizens, is dead. — *Bulletin*, Nov. 2d.

NOT DEAD. — Old Bummer still lives in spite of the murderous obituary notices written by those who have long disputed with him for precedence at the free lunch tables, and would be but too happy to count him out of the ring. He is worth a dozen of his would-be mourners yet. — *Alta*, Nov. 3d.

With its usual disregard for truth, the *Bulletin* of last evening announced poor old Bummer's death. But at last accounts he was still alive, and hopes were entertained for his recovery. — *Flag*, Nov. 3d.

A certain disreputable journal in this city impugns our reputation for veracity by asserting that we falsely reported Bummer's death. We again declare that Mr. Bummer died at three o'clock yesterday morning. Our informants are gentlemen of the highest standing and respectability. *Guillotine*.

Our reporters have just returned from the ranch at Hayes' Valley, where Bummer has gone to recuperate, and announce that that individual is greatly benefited by the change of air, diet, and scenery. Bummer still lives, in spite of the endeavors of a certain vile mercenary sheet in this city to kill him off. — *Flag*.

CONFIRMATORY. — "Bummer" has "gone to rusticate at Bessey's ranch, Hayes Valley." — *Dramatic Chronicle*.

BUMMER IS NOT DEAD. — We are glad that the false report of the death of Bummer afforded the *Bulletin* an opportunity of showing what it could do in the obituary notice line. — *Californian*.

Bummer expired at Bessey's place, near Hayes' Park, at four o'clock, Thursday afternoon. His skin has been whipped off, and will be stuffed by a taxidermist. *Call*, Nov. 4th.

After all this sympathy expressed for Bummer, about one hundred saloon keepers are outbidding each other for his skin. It is reported to be worth one thousand dollars a year to any place of public resort. The proprietors of the Russ, Lick, Occidental and Cosmopolitan Hotels want it. The What Cheer wants it. The Academy of Natural Sciences wants it. The Society of California Pioneers wants it. Dr. Rowell wants it. The Anatomical Museum wants it. Two sensation preachers want it. Setchell wants it. Wheatleigh wants it. Maguire wants it. The Young Men's Christian Association wants it. Gen. Halleck wants it. Judge Shepheard wants it. The New Mining Bureau wants it. The *Flag* and *Alta* are fighting for it.

> Great Bummer dead and turned to clay,
> Stops by no holes to keep the rats away.
> No longer now, they dread his crushing paws,
> Or view with horror his projecting jaws.

Unfortunately the files of many newspapers have not survived and we are left with tantalizing allusions to several lost stories, as indicated in the preceding summary of contemporary accounts in the Golden Era.

THE DAMON AND PYTHIAS OF SAN FRANCISCO.

55

Daily Morning Call.

JUMP UPON "BUMMER." — The best thing yet produced in respect to the memory of the late lamented "Bummer" is a lithograph by Jump, representing his unsouled tabernacle of clay lying in state. At each of the four corners of the platforms on which lies prone his mortal remains, stands a lighted candle, by the funereal glare of which the observer may discover divers rats cautiously approaching to look upon and insult their fallen foe, so human-like. The glare of these candles opens further discoveries. It enables one to see the spirit of "Lazarus" enjoying himself at free lunch. Many might think it is the real "Lazarus" that is there depicted; but it is not, gentle reader; 'tis only his spirit. "Lazarus" really don't need anything to eat now, since he is dead, and if you will watch that picture for years you will see that the spirit dog does not touch a morsel. The picture is purely allegorical, and is designed to teach children that when they sit down to the table they should not be too eager to begin eating. Children who have parents or guardians need not resort to the pictorial allegory to learn this propriety, although there is much to be learned from pictures. The appendant versification, entitled "The Damon and Pythias of San Francisco," is too touching to admit of more than one line being read at a time, and as there are over two hundred of these lines, the reader will have time to reflect as he goes along. It was a fine piece of witticism perpetrated by the author, when he called it "an elegiac, satirical poem, by Trem," (Delirium Trem.;) and another happy hit was in manufacturing a long string of ineffable doggerel, to celebrate the praises of one of "Bummer's" species.

The poem is reproduced in full beginning on page 67.

Daily Dramatic Chronicle.

SUNDAY, NOVEMBER 12, 1865

COWARDLY LITTLE "CALL."

Good kindly-hearted Bummer, the pet of the public, lies a corpse, and now, while the sorrow-stricken people bemoan his loss, the horrid, fiendish little *Call* publishes a paragraph which commences thus: "Jump upon Bummer." You'd like to jump upon him now he's dead, would you? You daren't do it while he was alive. "Jump upon Bummer!" Isn't this pretty advice to give to people who loved and respected him while alive, and now mourn his loss. We are not in favor of mob law, but—could it cause any surprise if an enraged populace demolished the office of the paper which dared to say "Jump upon Bummer." The remainder of the paragraph may possibly afford an explanation of the reasons the cowardly little *Call* has for saying "Jump upon Bummer," but we are sure that nothing can extenuate the barbarity of such advice. When we saw that first line it was enough for us—we threw down the *Call* in disgust and jumped upon that. We read no further; we hope we are not yet so hard up for reading matter as to be driven to read the local items of the *Call*.

Daily Evening Bulletin.

WEDNESDAY, NOVEMBER 8, 1865

IN MEMORY OF "BUMMER."—We have received from E. Jump a capital lithograph on letter sheet, entitled *Bummer and Lazarus, the Damon and Pythias of San Francisco.* It represents the lately deceased *Bummer*—who is dead sure enough, despite numerous statements contradictory to the original notice of his demise in the *Bulletin*—reposing upon a raised platform, as in life he lay slumbering upon the sidewalk of Clay or Montgomery streets, "his custom ever of an afternoon," his forepaws extended, and his lower jaws flat upon the board.

At each corner of the platform burns a wax taper, while a colony of delighted rats play around and under the hangings, yet dare not closely approach their old enemy even in death. In the cloudy prespective [sic] appears an idealized figure of the translated *Lazarus, Bummer's fides Achates,* in the act to seize a bite from the lunch table of the Canine Walhalla, while giving a side glance towards his noble friend. *Bummer's* portrait is as faithful as a photograph. Appended to the lithograph is an elegiac, satirical poem by "Trem," who owns a different sort of mousetrap from Bummer's, and who appropriately begins his elegy with a bit of dog-Latin.

Daily Dramatic Chronicle.

A CRITICAL EYE.

The art critic of the *Bulletin* in his notice of Jump's lithograph of Bummer, says he is represented as reposing on a raised platform, and "at each corner of the platform burns a wax taper." We object to this statement. How does he know those tapers are *wax*? We are inclined to believe they are tallow, and can state good and sufficient reasons for that belief, while the *Bulletin's* critic has positively nothing to support his statement that they are wax. One of them is guttering, and a rat is enjoying the gutter, as rats are up to do; wax candles don't gutter. If this art critic makes any more such rash statements he must be discharged. The critic says "Trem" appropriately commences his doggrel poem with a bit of dog-Latin. We hope it was not the same appreciation of the fitness of things that made the *Bulletin* call Lazarus "Bummer's *fides* Achates"—that is dog-Latin; but we are willing to believe that the printer and proof-reader are at fault. As "perspective" is turned into "prespective," the *Bulletin's* art critic for the occasion, who writes more correctly as a rule than nine-tenths of the editors in this city, very probably wrote "*fidus Achates.*" But the candles are *not* wax.

[page 2]

58

"BUMMER."

We have received from the publisher Mr. Jump's last, and in some respects his best, picture. It represents the illustrious Bummer dead and lying in state under funereal lights, with many an enfranchised rat rejoicing around the corpse of their old enemy. The portrait is perfect. In the vague perspective the shade of Lazarus is seen subjugating a free lunch. Printed on the same letter sheet with the lithograph is a lengthy elegiac, satirical poem by "Trem," in which a biography of Bummer is giving, [sic] together with some account of the budding, blooming, and blighting by death, of that singular affection between him and his friend Lazarus, which made both so famous on this coast.

[page 3]

Daily Morning Call.

SUNDAY, NOVEMBER 12, 1865

"BUMMER" AGAIN.— The good always have a place in our memories, and between the pen and the pencil, the writist and the artist, poor old dead "Bummer" is likely to be remembered many days as the type of well-behaved dogs. If his virtues have afforded a theme for the poetry sharp, so have the graces of his person supplied a subject for the man who makes cartoons. Jump waxeth enthusiastic over the dorg. He has produced a beautiful life-like portrait of "Bummer" as he used to lie out lazily on the sidewalk. The picture is exhibited in Roos's window, Russ House Block. Any one who ever had the slightest acquaintance with the subject of the picture, will recognize it at once.

THE CALIFORNIAN.

SATURDAY, NOVEMBER 11, 1865

THE *Flag* displays a mean jealousy of the dead dog "Bummer," and the honors paid to his memory. Surely, a dog who did so much towards exterminating rats may naturally be regretted in a city so cursed with them as is San Francisco; but, perhaps, the *Flag* may be prejudiced against him on this account. When the *Flag* dies, it cannot expect to be as much lamented as Bummer, for it has been in existence in this city but a very short time, and can scarcely, we should imagine, have the vanity to claim equality with Bummer, who, while he lived, did the city better service than the *Flag*, under its present management, would do in a century. Yet, if the *Flag* will die within any reasonable space of time—say, three weeks or a month—it shall not lack an epitaph.

[page 1]

"BUMMER'S" ELEGY.—"Bummer," whilom companion of "Lazarus," whose joint exploits, in the flesh, have been so long a solace to chronicler and reporter, even in death is not forgotten. Jump and "Trem" have, with pen and pencil, apotheosized the defunct canine, and their combined effort, on a letter sheet, is the latest sensation.

[page 9]

EXIT "BUMMER."—As we have devoted but little space to an event which has filled our local contemporaries with as much sorrow (judging from the columns of lamentations it has called forth) as would the decease of the best biped in the city, we give "Mark Twain's" view of the occurrence, as recorded in the ENTERPRISE of the 8th. Strangely enough, Mark, who can't stand "ballad infliction" seems to think there has not been quite enough of "Bummer":

"The old vagrant 'Bummer' is really dead at last; and although he was always more respected than his obsequious vassal, the dog 'Lazarus,' his exit has not made half as much stir in the newspaper world as signalised the departure of the latter. I think it is because he died a natural death: died with friends around him to smooth his pillow and wipe the death-damps from his brow, and receive his last words of love and resignation; because he died full of years, and honor, and disease, and fleas. *He* was permitted to die a natural death, as I have said, but poor Lazarus 'died with his boots on'—which is to say, he lost his life by violence; he gave up the ghost mysteriously, at dead of night, with none to cheer his last moments or soothe his dying pains. So the murdered dog was canonized in the newspapers, his shortcomings excused and his virtues heralded to the world; but his superior, parting with his life in the fullness of time, and in the due course of nature, sinks as quietly as might the mangiest cur among us. Well, let him go. In earlier days he was courted and caressed; but latterly he has lost his comeliness—his dignity had given place to a want of self-respect, which allowed him to practice mean deceptions to regain for a moment that sympathy and notice which had become necessary to his very existence, and it was evident to all that the dog had had his day: his great popularity was gone forever. In fact, Bummer should have died sooner: there was a time when his death would have left a lasting legacy of fame to his name. Now, however, he will be forgotten in a few days. Bummer's skin is to be stuffed and placed with that of Lazarus."

[page 12]

61

POOR OLD BUMMER!!

62

Daily Alta California.

POOR OLD BUMMER.— We have received a lithographic copy of a sketch by "Snooks, Jr.", with the above title. It embodies a large number of caricatures of well known San Franciscans, some of which, having been faithfully copied from Jump's efforts in that line, are remarkably good. To be frank, however, we must say that the sketch, as a whole, is a remarkable failure— what is good in it not being original, and what is original not worthy of mention. It is hardly necessary to say that Jump, who is really an artist of merit, had nothing to do with its production.

The signature on the lithograph reads S.Nooks, Jr.

Daily Morning Call.

"POOR OLD BUMMER."— Appleton has sent us a lithograph, of the caricature order, entitled as above, designed and executed by G.H. Baker. It represents the dead "Bummer" lying in state, surrounded by most of the notabilities of the city. The picture, as a whole, seems to be made up of the ideas expressed by Jump in several of his inimitable caricatures, combined into one. It makes quite a picture, but more noticeable for the many likenesses of well-known citizens it contains than for any originality of ideas or conception. Though a local notoriety and pet, "Bummer" was but a dog after all, and we do not admire the taste manifested in representing prominent divines and generals as among the most prominent of those paying respects to his remains. Jump's idea, in the little picture he has issued a few days ago, was much happier, and conceived in better taste, than the one in the picture before us.

Daily Morning Call.

WHAT SCREW IS LOOSE?—The *Bulletin* and *Alta* are at swords' points over the decision of the Supreme Court, in the Moses Frank case. Since the decease of their great prototypes, "Bummer" and "Lazarus," these journals manifest an unwonted disposition to quarrel. Why, is the matter beyond the ken of the people. So long as the original "Bummer" lived, the imitative "Lazarus"—*Alta*—followed faithfully in the footsteps of its illustrious prototype, and obeyed the behests of its "Bummer," the *Bulletin*. But as soon as the original "Bummer" shuffled off his canine coil, the imitator of "Lazarus" commenced a warfare with "Bummer's" shadow. Does the "Lazarus" of journalism imagine, that because *the* "Bummer" has departed, it can ride over its old file leader? Why is it, that as soon as the original "Bummer" and "Lazarus" are "gathered to their fathers," their journalistic namesakes commence such a bitter warfare as the one they are now waging over the Frank's case? Is it because the once proud and defiant leader and the once humble and meek follower has [sic] been retained by opposing parties? Why, in fact, does "Lazarus" bark in defiance of the Supreme Court, and "Bummer" growl and show his teeth in defence of that institution? In short, what great public interest or immense private speculation is at stake, to cause the *Bulletin* and *Alta* to fight each other as they do, and to impugn each others motives, because of a decision of the Supreme Court in a very common criminal case? Nothing but a powerful rival as well as private motive could induce the journalistic "Bummer" and "Lazarus" to growl and fight as fierce as they do over a subject which, upon its face, appears to exhibit no basis for public interest. One is compelled to believe that the *Alta* is especially interested in Frank's acquittal, and the *Bulletin* has as powerful an interest in securing his incarceration. Yet, why either should be so deeply concerned in the matter, can be accounted for only upon the supposition that both are greatly interested—though oppositely—in the crimes with which he is accused.

Epilogue

Many years later, in 1892, the *Call* reported that the stuffed skins of Bummer and Lazarus were to be exhibited at the 1893 World's Columbia Exposition in Chicago. More recent reports have indicated they were then displayed at the M. H. de Young Memorial Museum in San Francisco's Golden Gate Park. Elsewhere it has been suggested that the skins survived until 1906, when they were lost in the earthquake and fire that devastated the city.

However, I found no mention of them in the official list of exhibits printed in the *Final Report of the California World's Fair Commission* (Sacramento, 1894). Nor do I find any verification in the massive handwritten inventory books at the de Young. In fact, the last report of any substance is the one in the July 3, 1892, issue of the *Call*, wherein it is reported that at that particular time the skins were still on display in two of the saloons the dogs had frequented during their lifetimes: Lazarus at 425 Sansome (formerly Pless & Martin's) and Bummer at 534 Montgomery (formerly Martin & Horton's).

M.E.B.

Appendix A

The following poem was printed on a letter sheet illustrated by Edward Jump in November, 1865 (see page 55).

BUMMER AND LAZARUS
THE DAMON AND PYTHIAS OF SAN FRANCISCO

THEIR LIVES AND THEIR DEATHS. THEIR SEPARATION AND THEIR FINAL REUNION IN THE DOG STAR—THE PLACE WHERE GOOD DOGS GO.

AN ELEGIAC, SATIRICAL POEM
BY TREM

Cano canem honestatis
  Qui assumpsit carnem bonum gratis—
Now all must confess 'twould be quite the right thing
The praise of a dog in dog-Latin to sing
'Gainst the use of dead language sure nought can be said—
'Tis the right sort to write when one's praising the dead;
But as Bummer's translated, perhaps 'tis as well
For me to translate my dog-Latin, nor tell
In a language Americans understand least
My tale of a merry cur lately deceased.
Did I write it in Dutch,
Many hearts it would touch;

French, Spanish, Chinook or Kanaka—
  Why e'en in Chinese
  My story would please.
John would often give Bummer a cracker;
  Bummer, too kind to spurn
  Poor John's gift, in return
Made piratical raids on the ratteries;
  And as John likes rat pie,
  To repay him would try
By more than mere tail-wagging flatteries.
Bummer's no more on Clay street seen.
  Oh, cruel 'twas to say,

67

Raising false hopes by paradox,
  "Bummer's returned to clay."
Physic's no use thrown to the dogs,
  Yet for curtailed life
It oft is held responsible;
  Some sad reports were rife—
'Twas said that one who Bummer loved
  Sought him where he did lie,
And brought physicians to his aid—
  To help the dog to die.
'Tis false! Kind hands supplied his wants
  With savory mutton broth—
No Angel Death in doctor's guise
  For him poured vials of wrath.

Of Bummer's birth and parentage
  There's litterally nothing known,
If he one of a litter was,
  Or if he entered life alone;
    Who was his father,
      Who was his mother,
    It's not worth while
      One's head to bother.
There's many a worthy Pioneer
Whose history commences here;
  Who's proud of this State,
  Doesn't care to relate

The events of his life seriatim.
  One who if he meet
  An old friend in the street,
Who *knows* him would fain spiflicate him,
  Proud enough is the boast
  That he came to this coast
In the early times—good times for miners,
  Let new-comers give way!
  'Tis enough—he can say,
"I was one of the old '49-ers!"

Bummer came 'cross the Plains, a bold pioneer;
Reached Sacramento in the spring of the year;
Stood the heat for a while, but one very hot Summer
It became so terrific that really poor Bummer
  Concluded his brain,
  If he there should remain,
  Would certainly bake,
  So concluded to take
  A cool leave of the city—
While there he was really a subject for pity.
  Lunch tables up there
  Set very poor fare—
  Crackers, cabbage and cheese
  Of course could not please

A dog, who, like Bummer, knew good grub from bad.
He besides was quite nervous—he feared he'd go mad
From the heat, so concluded 'twas best he should go by a
Steamer to 'Frisco t'escape hydrophobia.
   When Bummer came here
     He soon saw the cats
Of this city knew nothing
     About killing rats,
And in a few days
     Made all understand
That rat-killing biz
     Was right in his hand.
"Paws" perhaps would be better—to pause and correct,
A faux pas in this doggerel no one can expect
   Me to trouble myself.
     I won't if I know it
Make many false rhymes—
     Although not a poet,
I've mounted my Pegasus, now let her go it!
   Bummer and rats I sing!
     Oh, heavenly muse,
   To sing of slaught'ring rats
     Pray don't refuse—
Thousands of "poets" bid thee tune thy notes,
To sing of bipeds cutting bipeds' throats.
For feats of valor my four-footed hero
Was famed, and shed much blood as ancient Nero;

Lives forfeited by theft did Bummer take;
He's seize a rat and, with earthquake-like shake,
Shake out its life, then drop the empty case,
And after other victims go in chase.

A dog of some substance now Bummer became;
His merit acknowledged, he soon achieved fame;
To the market for dinner he'd go, after work,
And each butcher would spare him sparerib of pork,
   Or a nice tenderloin,
     Which Bummer to coin
   Preferred to a steak.
   And gladly would take
     His game to keep going.
Thus Bummer would often in going his rounds
Receive enough food for a full pack of hounds.
Mete reward for his labors, for Bummer ne'er vermin ate,
Though he worked night and day the whole race to
   exterminate.

I am sorry to say that some dogs are like men—
There are mongrel curs who are envious when
A dog by his merit attains a "posish"
In the eyes of the world, and most heartily wish
That he'll some day just swallow a bone while he's
feeding;

But none envied Bummer, save dogs of ill breeding.
  Two-legged bummers a few
  Rather envied him, too;
  They'd growl out—"D--n,
  In men's estimation,
  It is quite plain to see,
  That far higher than we
Stands that four-legged bummer. Oh! why should this be?"
  Thus we oft see inferiors
  Envy superiors—
  But Bummer was kind,
  To their faults he was blind;
  None accused him of putting
On airs, but, as if they stood on equal footing,
  He'd recognize 'tothers,
  And treat them as brothers,
  Though all men confessed
  That his standing was best,
  For respected was he
  By the community.

Bummer was strong, and Bummer was bold;
Bummer would never stand by and behold
Two dogs set on one—for 'tisn't fair play;
Bummer in such cases had a say.

  A cowardly sight
  Met his gaze one night:
  Big dogs a score,
  Or maybe more,
Were biting, and shaking, and pulling, and kickin'
A poor thin young dog who was weak as a chicken.
Bummer was angry, Bummer got hot;
Bummer just went in and cleaned out the lot,
And he howled in a rage, as off they slunk:
"A cowardly dog is as mean as a skunk!"
The poor weak dog, who was yellow and black,
With his four legs up, lay flat on his back.
  Bummer helped him up,
  This poor weak pup,
  Rubbed his poor paws,
  Licked all his sores,
And invited the poor devil home to sup.
He shared his bones, he shared his bread—
If he'd had such a thing he'd have shared his bed;
But this treat he could not his sick friend give,
For the street was where Bummer did sleep and live.
The public were pleased with Bummer's behavior,
And the black and tan canine quite worshiped his savior.
The public named him Lazarus, because
Dog Bummer had come and licked his sores.
Bummer and Lazarus made a pair
At which all strangers in town would state,

And some two-legged bummer would tell the story,
Which covered Bummer with endless glory.
The world wagged on and Bummer, though fat,
Would semi-occasionally tackle a rat.
Bummer did the killing, Laz. the bragging;
Standing by, his tail incessantly wagging,
He'd take his share of caresses and pats,
And seem to say, "Can't *we* kill rats!"
It happened on one fatal day
Laz. from Bummer chanced to stray,
Chanced a bone to fix his eyes on—
Bone looked nice—'twas smeared with pison!!
 Lazarus picked the bone,
 Lay down—gave a groan;
 Fatal want of caution!
 A horrible contortion
 His mild face disfigured;
 Small boy said, "I'm jiggered,
 If Laz. aint a goner!"
 (Small boy's name was Horner.)
'Twas even so—Laz. was dead;
Many a bitter tear was shed.
Next day Bummer, reckless, tried
To end his life by suicide,
Lay down on the railroad track,
Flat upon his big broad back.
Fate refused his offering votive—

Stoker stopped the locomotive.
Bummer each day grew sadder and sadder;
Sighing and grief blew him up like a bladder:
As it did poor Jack Falstaff, 'twill cause no surprise
That a grief-swollen body is known by its sighs.
 On the second of November,
 A day we'll long remember,
 Poor old Bummer, swol'n with grief,
 (Wicked wretches say 'twas beef,)
 Breathed his last expiring sigh,
 Went to join his friend on high—
 Went where brightly shines afar
 Sirius, the good Dog Star.
 A grand previsionary dream
 He had the day he died—it seemed
That Laz., his friend long loved now dead,
Stood by a rich celestial spread;
"Provisions see," he seemed to say,
"Brother Bummer, haste away;
Here dogs always have their day.
Prithee, friend, no longer stay!"
A gleam of joy o'er Bummer's face
 Shone brightly—he was gone!
None can ever fill his place;
 The city's left forlorn!

Appendix B

The *Daily Alta California* (1849-1891) began as a weekly but, on January 22, 1850, became San Francisco's first daily newspaper. During the period of our story the *Alta* published four regular editions—a daily (every morning, except Mondays*) for circulation in the city; an evening (except Sundays) for circulation in the interior; a weekly (Thursdays); and also the *Steamer Alta California* which was printed expressly for the Eastern states and Europe, to be carried there by steam ship via the Horn.

Until 1872 there were not any newspapers in the city on Monday mornings.

Daily Evening Bulletin (1855-1929) was established by James King of William and, for many years it had the largest circulation in the city. It also published a weekly edition (Saturdays), and a steamer edition. In 1929 it was sold to William Randolph Hearst who merged it with the *Call*.

The *Daily Morning Call* (1856-1965). Samuel Clemens was the Washoe (Nevada) correspondent for this paper in 1863, and for a brief period in 1864 he worked for it as a reporter in San Francisco. The paper changed hands a number of times and in 1929 it was merged with the *Bulletin*. The *Call-Bulletin* was absorbed by the *Examiner* in 1965.

The Golden Era (1852-1893) was more of a literary publication than a newspaper. Although it often printed summaries of news items from local papers it concentrated on short stories and serialized versions of new sensational novels.

The Californian (1864-1866) was another literary magazine in newspaper format. Samuel Clemens often wrote for it, using his pseudonym Mark Twain. Ambrose Bierce and Bret Harte were among other regular contributors. Its tone was more lighthearted than that of *The Golden Era.*

The *Daily Dramatic Chronicle* (1865-   ) was a free four-page paper devoted primarily to news and announcements of the local theater scene. It was established in January, 1865, by seventeen-year-old Michael de Young and his twenty-year-old brother, Charles. The youths had borrowed $20 to begin the venture. In 1868 it was converted to a regular news paper, the *Daily Morning and Evening Chronicle.* Today, as the *San Francisco Chronicle,* it is the city's leading morning paper.

The Daily Examiner (1865-   ) is the only other newspaper of the period still being published. It first appeared in July, 1865—a few months before Bummer died. George Hearst bought it in 1880 and used it to further his own political career before giving it to his son, William Randolph Hearst. Today it is the *San Francisco Examiner*—the city's afternoon paper.

Glossary

page

2   *Daily Alta California:* The newspaper bears the early Spanish name for what is today known as California. In 1804 the Spanish territory north of Mexico was divided into *Baja California* (lower California) and *Alta California* (upper California). The Spanish word, *alta* (upper; above), is used again on page 64 when referring to the deceased Lazarus as *Alta Lazarus.*

25   *cur non?:* A dual-language pun. As Latin, the phrase means "why not?" Reading the first word as English, one gets "...and not a cur?"

26   *Damon and Pythias:* The names of two Pythagorean philosophers of the fourth century B.C. whose steadfast friendship for each other had become proverbial.

33   *The Consolidation Act:* This Act (April, 1860) consolidated the government of the city and county of San Francisco within newly established boundaries.

page

33   *cartes de visite:* (French) A small photographic portrait mounted on card, 3-1/2″ x 2-1/2″. Also a visiting card.

33   *Mayhew:* An allusion to Edward Mayhew's book, *Dogs and Their Management,* which was first published in 1858 and went through twenty-three printings before being revised in 1897.

34   *Major Bagstock:* A character in Charles Dickens' *Dombey and Son.*

36   *Gilmore's Swamp Angel:* This would have been a topical reference to the gun invented by Robert Parker Parrott and used against Charleston, North Carolina, during the Civil War. The weapon was nicknamed "The Swamp Angel of General Gilmore."

37   *Lazarus redivivus:* (Latin) "Lazarus alive again" Refers to the brother of Martha and Mary, whom Jesus raised from the dead (John 11. 1-44) and not to the beggar of the parable in Luke 16. 19-31.

37 *Martin Farquhar Tupper* was an English writer whose phenomenal popularity on both sides of the Atlantic in the 1840s and 1850s was followed by a humiliating barrage of ridicule and criticism. His *Proverbial Philosophy* (1838) was a collection of moralizing and patriotic verses which at first were quoted with reverence and later scorned as verbiage. When the Princess Alexandra of Denmark arrived in London in 1863 to marry the Prince of Wales (they succeeded Queen Victoria in 1901 as King Edward VII and Queen Alexandra), Tupper wrote this gushing welcome:

A hundred thousand Welcomes!
A hundred thousand Welcomes,
   And a hundred thousand more!
O happy heart of England,
Shout aloud, and sing, land,
   As no land sang before!
   And let the paean soar
   And ring from shore to shore
A hundred thousand Welcomes,
   And a hundred thousand more!
   And let the cannons roar
   The joy-stunn'd city o'er,
   And let the steeples chime it
A hundred thousand Welcomes,
   And a hundred thousand more,—
   And let the people rhyme it

   From neighbour's door to door,
   From every man's heart's core,—
A hundred thousand Welcomes,
   And a hundred thousand more!

This became a particular favorite for parody in America as well as in England—as "100,000 Pities" further testifies.

47 *in articulo mortis:* (Latin) Legal and medical jargon meaning "at point of death."

48 *memento mori:* (Latin) "remember that you shall die" This thought, expressed here in the Latin of the Roman poet Horace, was a favorite theme of Greek and Roman writers. Various morals were drawn from it: make the most of your joys, for they are brief; overcome your sorrow, for it too will end; be not too proud, for you are not immortal.

50 *quondam:* (Latin) "former"

56 *Delirium Trem.:* an allusion to *delirium tremens*— "trembling madness"—the medical Latin for a violent delirium with tremors, induced by excessive and prolonged use of alcohol.

58 *fides Achates:* (Latin) The phrase as used here is either intended as hendiadys (loyalty = Achates), or is in error for *fidus Achates* (q.v.).

58 *fidus Achates:* (Latin) "loyal Achates," in Virgil's *Aeneid,* the faithful companion of the hero Aeneas. In the European literary tradition Achates became a synonym for a loyal friend, and the *American Heritage Dictionary* still has an entry under "Achates" with the generic definition "a loyal friend."

67 *cano canem honestatis/qui assumpsit carnem bonum gratis:* (Latin) "I sing of a dog of respectability, who picked up fine meat for free." The line echoes the opening of Virgil's *Aeneid (Arma virumque cano*—Of arms and the man I sing) but uses, or rather abuses, the meter of a medieval hymn tune. There is a pun in the first two words, which may be rendered "I write doggerel about a dog...."

Bibliography

Newspapers and magazines

Daily Alta California
1860: 2-4; 4-21.
1861: 1-18; 4-12; 9-12.
1862: 4-22; 5-13; 6-14; 6-16; 6-17 (2); 6-24; 10-3.
1863: 2-14; 2-17; 7-13; 10-27.
1864: 1-12; 2-28.
1865: 9-14; 10-9; 11-5; 11-15.

Daily Evening Bulletin
1862: 5-1; 5-7; 5-13; 5-14; 6-11; 6-17; 10-22.
1863: 10-3; 10-26.
1864: 8-25.
1865: 9-15; 11-3; 11-8.
1893: 11-25.
1913: 12-20; 12-27.
1914: 1-3.

Daily Morning Call
1864: 7-31.
1865: 10-11; 11-2; 11-4; 11-8 (2); 11-12; 11-15.
1880: 1-9.
1892: 7-3.

Daily Dramatic Chronicle
1865: 11-3; 11-10 (2); 11-12.

The Daily Examiner
1865: 11-3; 11-4.

The Californian
1865: 11-11 (3).

Golden Era
1865: 11-5 (2).

The Argonaut
v.10. no.4. Jan. 28, 1882. ''Bummer and Lazarus.
A San Francisco Sketch.'' Margaret Hosmer. (*Lippincott*,
February.)

The Overland Monthly
v.19. (Second Series.) no. 113. May, 1892.
''Street Characters of San Francisco.'' Francis E. Sheldon.
v.58. no.3. Sept., 1911. Poem by Fred Emerson Brooks.

Books
The following books provided information:

The San Francisco Directory. 1861 through 1870.

Final Report of the California World's Fair Commission.
Sacramento. 1894.

San Francisco Theatre Research. v.15, pt.1. pp 160/61. Work Projects Administration. 1940.

Martin Tupper. His Rise and Fall. Derek Hudson. Constable, London. 1949.

Cithara. Martin F. Tupper. Virtue Brothers & Co., London. 1863.

Bummer and Lazarus. An Historical Dog Story. A small monograph in library of The Society of California Pioneers, San Francisco. No indication as to author, publisher, or date of publication. Possibly printed In 1890s.

A Companion to California. James D. Hart. Oxford University Press, New York. 1978.

Clemens of the 'Call'. Mark Twain in San Francisco. Edited by Edgar M. Branch. University of California Press. 1969.

Gaudy Century. John Bruce. Random House, New York. 1948.

Other books and publications containing references to Bummer and Lazarus:

The Memorable Lives of Bummer & Lazarus. (Citizens of San Francisco) 185?-1865. Anne Bancroft. The Ward Ritchie Press. 1939. (500 copies)

The Forgotten Characters of Old San Francisco. Robert Ernest Cowan, Anne Bancroft, and Addie L. Ballou. The Ward Ritchie Press. 1964. (Includes reprint of *The Memorable Lives of Bummer & Lazarus*.)

Emperor Norton. Life and Experiences of a Notable Character in San Francisco. 1849-1880. Edited by Albert Dressler. Albert Dressler. 1927.

San Francisco's Emperor Norton "I." David Warren Ryder. David Warren Ryder. 1939.

Emperor Norton. Mad Monarch of America. Allen Stanley Lane. The Caxton Printers Ltd., Caldwell, Idaho. 1939.

San Francisco Kaleidoscope. Samuel Dickson. Stanford University Press. 1949.

Tales of San Francisco. Samuel Dickson. Stanford University Press. 1957. (Includes reprint of *San Francisco Kaleidoscope*.)

The San Francisco Stage. A History. Edmond M. Cagey. Columbia University Press, New York. 1950.

San Francisco Magic City. Mrs. Fremont Older (Cora Older) Longmans, Green & Co. 1961.

Our City: The Jews of San Francisco. Irena Narell. Howell-North Publishers, Inc. San Diego. 1981.

EDWARD JUMP was born in France in 1832 and, at the age of 20, immigrated to California in search of gold. After futile attempts at the mines he settled in San Francisco and soon gained fame as a well respected satirical cartoonist. His artistic talents were honed while working with local publisher James Hutchings and lithographers Benjamin Butler and Louis Nagel. His cartoons were sold either as individual lithographs or as letter sheets, a popular form of stationery illustrated with drawings of local scenes or events, often with lengthy descriptions. His work also appeared in the national magazine *Puck* and as advertisements in other publications.

He left San Francisco in the late 1860s and returned briefly to Paris before moving to Washington, D.C. There he shared accommodations at a boarding house with Mark Twain, who later announced that the two of them would be collaborating on a book about the Sandwich Islands (Hawaii). Sadly, this did not happen.

Jump married and moved to Montreal, then to New Orleans, St. Louis and other cities before settling in Chicago in 1880. On April 21, 1883, drunk and despondent at being ordered out of his boarding house, Edward Jump shot and killed himself in the office of his publisher.

MALCOLM E. BARKER was born in London and immigrated to San Francisco in 1961 after first visiting that city while working in the purser's office on the cruise ship *Iberia*. Before leaving England he had worked as a newspaper reporter, and also as the assistant press officer of Thomas Cook travel agency. He became an American citizen in 1983. One year later he formed Londonborn Publications in order to produce the original *Bummer & Lazarus: San Francisco's Famous Dogs*. Other books he has published are: *Book design & production for the small publisher* (1990), *San Francisco Memoirs 1835-1851: Eyewitness accounts of the birth of a city* (1994), *More San Francisco Memoirs: 1852-1899, The ripening years* (1996), and *Three Fearful Days: San Francisco Memoirs of the 1906 earthquake & fire* (1998).

OTHER BOOKS BY MALCOLM E. BARKER

San Francisco Memoirs 1835-1851: Eyewitness accounts of the birth of a city

"There's a very real feeling of authenticity in this book . . . some wonderful reading."
                                        KKSF-FM radio
$16.95 Paperback. 6 x 9. 320 pages.
ISBN 0-930235-04-5

More San Francisco Memoirs: 1852-1899 The ripening years

"All the events and issues that give San Francisco its unique character, for better or worse . . . are here."
                              San Francisco Chronicle
$16.95 Paperback. 6 x 9. 320 pages.
ISBN 0-930235-05-3

Three Fearful Days: San Francisco Memoirs of the 1906 earthquake & fire

"I recommend this book to anyone who plans to read only one book about the 1906 earthquake."
                  Institute for Historical Study Newsletter
$16.95 Paperback. 6 x 9. 336 pages.
ISBN 0-930235-06-1

Check your local bookstore.
Or order direct from Londonborn Publications with payment including shipping ($2.50 for first title plus $1.00 for each additional title).

Londonborn Publications
P.O. Box 77246, San Francisco, 94107-0246
website: wwwsanfranciscomemoirs.com

Index

1984

Book and cover design: Malcolm E. Barker.
Text typeface: Bookman Light, set by Pat Young
at Hillside Setting, Novato, California.
Display matter: Chisel (title), Wide Latin, Bold Latin, and
miscellaneous typefaces similar to original newspaper
mastheads—handset by Malcolm E. Barker at Feathered
Serpent Press, San Rafael, California.

2001

Cover design: David R. Johnson.
Copy editor: Jackie Pels, Hardscratch Press.
Text typeface of new material: Bookman and Wide
Latin.
Text paper: 60-lb. Glatfelter Offset.
Printed and bound by Thomson-Shore, Inc.,
Dexter, Michigan